Brooke Foss Westcott

The Revelation of the risen Lord

Brooke Foss Westcott

The Revelation of the risen Lord

ISBN/EAN: 9783743347618

Manufactured in Europe, USA, Canada, Australia, Japa

Cover: Foto ©ninafisch / pixelio.de

Manufactured and distributed by brebook publishing software (www.brebook.com)

Brooke Foss Westcott

The Revelation of the risen Lord

THE REVELATION

OF THE

RISEN LORD.

THE REVELATION

OF THE

RISEN LORD.

BY

BROOKE FOSS WESTCOTT, D.D., D.C.L.,

REGIUS PROFESSOR OF DIVINITY, CAMBRIDGE,
CANON OF PETERBOROUGH,
AND CHAPLAIN IN ORDINARY TO THE QUEEN.

London and Cambridge:
MACMILLAN AND CO.
1881

ΤΊ ΖΗΤΕῖΤΕ ΤῸΝ ΖῶΝΤΑ ΜΕΤᴀ ΤῶΝ ΝΕΚΡῶΝ; ΟΫ̓Κ
ἔCTIN ὧΔΕ ἀλλὰ ἬΓΕΡΘΗ.

Why seek ye the Living among the dead? He is not here but is risen.

LUKE xxiv. 6.

	PAGE
Contents	iii
Preface	ix

INTRODUCTORY.

THE GENERAL CHARACTER OF THE REVELATION AND OF THE RECORD.

The fact of the Resurrection assumed 4

1. The Record of the Revelation of the Risen Christ

　fragmentary 5
　yet comprehensive 6

2. The Revelation

　(a)　discloses a new life 7
　　　Christ changed 8
　　　yet the same 9
　(β)　made to believers 10
　　　and this of necessity 10

I.

THE REVELATION THROUGH LOVE.

Two groups of the Manifestations of the Risen Lord . . . 18
The discipline of human love 20
The confession of love welcomed and interpreted . . . 22
The message of the Resurrection *I ascend* 24
Present importance of this first revelation 26

APPENDIX TO I.

The appearances to the women and to Mary Magdalene . . 33

II.

THE REVELATION THROUGH THOUGHT.

	PAGE
The general relation of the appearance to the disciples to that to Mary Magdalene	43
The two disciples unknown	45
Their spiritual position	46
Their thoughts called out and answered	48
The lesson of the manifestation	50
fulfilled in our own experience	52
The Resurrection interprets all life	54

III.

THE CONVICTION OF FAITH.

The manifestation of the Risen Christ to the Society	62
The presence of disbelief	64
Belief gained with difficulty;	65
but once gained it became the power of a new life	66
The Risen Christ truly man	68
A vision of St Martin	70
The permanent lesson of the Revelation	72

IV.

THE GREAT COMMISSION.

The record of St John the complement of the record of St Luke	80
The great Commission the charter of the Church	82
The relation of the mission of the Church to the mission of Christ	84
The work of the Church in fulfilment of Christ's mission	86

V.

SPIRITUAL SIGHT.

	PAGE
The test proposed by incredulity	96
A pause for thought	98
Christ's return	99
The discovery of Faith the blessing of the later Church	100
The starting-point and the end of Faith	102
Doubts affected and faced	104
Hearing and sight	106

VI.

THE REVELATION IN THE WORK OF LIFE.

Character of the second group of revelations of the Risen Lord	111
Work and experience old and new	114
The revelation gained by the interpretation of acts	116
Christ seen in His acts by Faith	118
The conditions of waiting	119
working and obedience	120

VII.

THE REVELATION THROUGH ACTIVE WORK.

Two forms of service	128
The charge to St Peter	130
The trial of the last question	131
St Peter's life the type of active service	132
in love, thoughtfulness and self-surrender	134
St Peter's martyrdom	136

VIII.
THE REVELATION THROUGH PATIENT WAITING.

	PAGE
The Coming of the Lord	142
Following and waiting	143
The silence of St John's life	144
Waiting a true service	146
needed at present	148

IX.
THE REVELATION OF THE KINGDOM.

The 'Mountain' the scene of the revelation	156
A Kingdom of all nations	158
Teaching interprets the first gift	160
Christ present all the days	161
The lessons of His abiding Presence	162
Power to be used	164
Note on [St Mark] xvi. 15—18; St Luke xxiv. 44—49	169

X.
DEPARTURE IN BLESSING.

The period of forty days	176
The intervals after the Baptism and the Resurrection	177
The Resurrection shewn in its glory by the Ascension	178
The Ascension an end and a beginning	180
Last words	182
Gone yet given for ever	183

XI.
THE REVELATION FROM HEAVEN AND ON EARTH.

The personal appearances of the Risen Lord come to a decisive close	192
till the unique appearance to St Paul	193
This appearance a revelation: Christ in heaven and on earth	194
A revelation of power in weakness	196
The type of the common miracle of life	198

THE following short studies are intended to serve as an Introduction or a Supplement to *The Gospel of the Resurrection*. It has been my aim in writing them to realise as distinctly as I could the characteristic teaching of each manifestation of the Risen Christ both in relation to the first disciples and in relation to ourselves. The result is, I think, to place in a fuller light the circumstances under which the fact of the Resurrection was apprehended and the nature of the fact itself. The different narratives when examined together leave no room for the growth of faith in a delusion; and they shew adequately how the import of the new Truth was grasped. They enable us to understand historically, and this we may expect to have made clear, how the Apostles, starting from the views of the Person and Work of Christ which they had gained while they followed His earthly ministry, checked for a brief space by the unexpected blow of the Passion, had their conceptions transfigured; and how the Christian Church was founded on the belief in the Ascended Lord.

At the same time a patient endeavour to enter into the meaning of the several recorded incidents brings out the absolute originality and the prevailing power of the Truth which they combine to make known. The idea of the Resurrection was a new thing; and it is seen to produce the effects of a new force.

The Fact of the Resurrection as thus set before us explains the Life of the Church; and the Fact itself, or the belief in the Fact, is not explicable by any antecedent conditions apart from its truth. A careful study of the evangelic records shews that there were no elements present in the society of the believers to produce such an idea as they slowly realised. There was no enthusiastic hope to create visions; still less to create visions which involved the sacrifice of cherished expectations. Everywhere it appears that a new thought is kindled by the successive manifestations of the Lord, for which earlier belief offered a sufficient foundation but no more.

In this connexion the remarkable limitation of the manifestations of the Risen Lord must be noticed. When 'the lesson of the new Life was once given it was not repeated. The revelation to St Paul, the revelation of 'Jesus' as 'the Son of God', completes the whole series. The visions of St Stephen and St John were of a different order.

The mode in which this new thought is presented strengthens the conviction that it could not have arisen spontaneously among the disciples. The Lord is revealed without any outward accompaniments of glory, and yet He brings with Him the effect of glory. There are no descriptions, as in later legendary histories, of any exceptional exercise of His power. All that He does is presented as the manifestation of a true, uniform, life. The contrasts which mark His entrance into the conditions of earthly existence are uniformly noticed without emphasis and without surprise. We are led to see that when the disciples reflected upon the scriptural promises of the Christ, and on their own earlier experience, the revelation of Jesus, alive after death for evermore, wholly changed and wholly the same, was in the truest sense of the word natural, a clear fulfilment of the one will of God.

It is not strictly correct therefore to say that the first disciples believed simply on the testimony of their senses. What they were able to see was the occasion of their belief, which rose beyond conclusions capable of being brought to such a test. And in the same way it is not strictly correct to say that we believe simply on the testimony of the Gospels. The narratives which have been handed down to us furnish us with a record of external phenomena which we examine in connexion with the unfolding of that which is seen to be a vast discipline of the world, and with the experience of individual souls. The idea of the Resurrection once given justifies itself. It is, it may be said, an interpretation, but it is the only adequate interpretation of the manifold phenomena which are set before us, confirmed by the life of Christ, by the life of men, by the life of man.

The presupposition of Faith is that there is a Divine goal and progress in life.

In the case of the first disciples this presupposition took the form of a belief in the Messianic promises embodied in the Jewish Scriptures and the Jewish history. At present it embraces a wider scope, and acknowledges that a 'growing purpose' can be seen in the whole discipline of the world. The conviction that the Messianic hope was fulfilled in Jesus of Nazareth enabled the apostles to enter into the meaning of the Cross, and through that of a spiritual kingdom.

The conviction that signs of a providential guidance are visible in the past records of humanity, pointing to man's capacity for divine fellowship, enable us to grasp the fact of the accomplishment of man's destiny in the Mission of the Son of God.

This wider view of the bearings of the Resurrection places its essential character in a true light. It is not properly an overwhelming fact attesting doctrines separate from itself, but a revelation which illuminates the whole range of human experience, all that we hear and see and feel. In this respect the Resurrection, like the Incarnation, must be regarded in relation to the divine idea of man as created in the image of God to gain the likeness of God, as well as in relation to the actual condition of man as fallen. It is in the latter connexion a beginning, a new creation, and in the former a consummation. The Incarnation gives the absolute pledge of the fulfilment of man's destiny: the Resurrection shews that fulfilment already attained, as far as our present powers enable us to realise the truth. So it is that Christ, as raised from the dead, is spoken of as 'the second Adam', in whom men are reborn, and also as 'the head of the body, the Church'. The Resurrection, as answering to death, so far depended on the Fall; but the glory of the Risen Lord, answering to the accomplishment of the idea in which man was created, is independent of it. We see in the Risen Christ the end for which man was made and the assurance that the end is within reach. The Resurrection, if we may so speak, shews us the change which would have passed over the earthly life of man, if sin had not brought in death.

This view of the significance of the Resurrection throws light upon problems which are now coming into sight. In the Risen Christ we see a type of humanity which is free from the accidents of time and place, while it embraces with living sympathy each fragmentary type. By dwelling upon such a spectacle we come to see the practical consequences of the truth which is guarded (though with imperfections which cling to human thoughts) by the doctrine that the personality of the Lord lies in His divine nature, so that in His humanity the separate individualities of men find a supreme unity.

A further advantage is likely to follow from a closer study of the manifestation of Christ thus brought before us. It will forcibly remind us that our belief is in a Risen and glorified Saviour. The earliest form of confession which was simply *'Jesus is Lord'*, embodies the truth which we are in danger of forgetting. Our endeavour must be not to recal the past work of Christ with the most vivid power, but to realise His present union with His Church. The fact of the Resurrection passes into the personal fellowship which He has established through His Spirit.

No one can study with concentrated attention any particular aspect of the revelation contained in Holy Scripture, influenced it may be by personal tendencies, without fearing that he may have limited in some degree the breadth and freedom of the original record. As far as this is the case he will be the first to deplore the error and to warn others against supposing that a clear and harmonious view of the elements of truth is necessarily a complete view. He will certainly have learnt and be anxious to affirm that what he endeavours to set forth is the result of listening to the very words of the Bible, and that his power of apprehension is no measure of the fulness of the divine message.

I am the more anxious to insist upon this truth, and to claim its application to all that I have written, because at the present stage in the progress of religious thought we seem to need above all things to enter with a living sympathy into the whole teaching of the Bible, in its many parts and many forms; to realise with a historical, no less than with a spiritual insight, what lessons it conveys and in what shape; in order that so we may be trained to recognise and to interpret the fresh lessons which the One Spirit is offering to us in other ways.

The earliest scene of the first Easter Day finds not unfrequently a parallel in our own experience. We go, perhaps with costly offerings, to seek the Lord in the sepulchre. Happy shall we be if we welcome the reproof which lifts our thoughts to the realities of a higher world: *Why seek ye the living among the dead? He is not here, but is risen.*

BUXTON,
Sept. 5, 1881.

INTRODUCTORY.

THE GENERAL CHARACTER OF THE REVELATION AND OF THE RECORD.

Ἔτι μικρὸν καὶ ὁ κόσμος με οὐκέτι θεωρεῖ, ὑμεῖς δὲ θεωρεῖτέ με, ὅτι ἐγὼ ζῶ καὶ ὑμεῖς ζήσετε.

Yet a little while, and the world beholdeth me no more; but ye behold me: because I live, ye shall live also.

JOHN xiv. 19.

THE GENERAL CHARACTER OF THE REVELATION AND OF THE RECORD.

IN the following chapters I propose to consider the various records of the manifestations of the Risen Christ which have been preserved in the Gospels, so far as they give us a revelation of His Being and His Work, so far as they help us to gain a right view of His unchanged Person; to apprehend, according to the measure of our powers, the conditions of that glorified human life on which He has entered; to understand more vitally the fact and the mode of His abiding Presence; to rise, if it may be, to a more energetic conception of the real union of the seen and the unseen which He has established and made known. In doing this it is not my object primarily to meet difficulties or to attempt to prove an article of our common faith. I wish at first to go back in feeling to the first Easter Morning, and then to trace again, as the Evangelists have traced for us, the growth of the new great thought of life which was on that day given to the world till it was held in its fulness. I wish to learn, and, as I may be enabled, to point

INTRODUC-
TORY.

1—2

out, the meaning of each detail in the several narratives of the Lord's appearance. I wish to ponder and to wait where light has not yet come. Such a course of patient reflection brings an assurance deeper and more abiding than any answer to isolated objections. It places the whole history before the student in the power of life; and the sense of life carries him beyond the limits of the letter.

But before entering upon the examination of the separate Evangelic records, it will be necessary to notice some of the features which mark the whole history. And it must never be forgotten that the history is not a history of the Resurrection, but a history of the manifestation of the Risen Christ. The fact of the Resurrection is assumed, but it is nowhere described. A veil lies over all beginnings. When this original limitation of the subject is firmly held, we have still to endeavour to apprehend the general conditions under which the revelation was made, and the general form in which it has been preserved, in order that we may be able afterwards to understand better the constituent parts of it.

We have, then, to consider the character of the revelation itself, and the character of the record of the revelation.

1. It will be most convenient to take the

second point first. And in regard to the record of the revelation, we cannot but be struck, as everywhere in the memorials of Christ's work, by observing how little is told us of all that was known. Of the forty days during which the Lord was seen, how few, five or six perhaps, can be connected with any vision. Of all the *things* which He *spake concerning the Kingdom of God*, how few sentences, so far as we know, have been committed to writing. Of the light which He poured upon the Scriptures *concerning Himself, beginning from Moses and from all the prophets*, how few rays have been preserved for the illumination and kindling of our hearts.

Or again, if we seek to make a connected picture of the events of the first Easter Day, and to arrange the several scenes in due connexion of time and place, it is at once evident that there are great chasms in our knowledge, and we learn patience in regard to that which is uncertain or perplexing. We perceive that the difficulties by which the outward history is beset spring from the abundant fulness of circumstances of which we know only isolated fragments. Here and there glimpses are given of facts which are not described, of an appearance to St Peter, of an appearance to St James. And elsewhere we feel that silence was almost a necessity. It was not,

Margin: INTRODUCTORY. Acts i. 3. Luke xxiv. 27. Luke xxiv. 24; 1 Cor. xv. 7.

INTRODUC-TORY.

for example, for us to read how the Divine Son in His glory met the Mother who had watched His long agony on the Cross.

But while the record of the earthly manifestations of the Risen Lord is thus fragmentary, each fragment is at the same time found to be instructive with its peculiar lesson. This will be seen more plainly afterwards. Now it will be enough to observe that there is the greatest variety in the circumstances of the recorded manifestations. The Lord appears to one and to many: to the loving, the waiting, the desponding, the doubtful: in the garden, on the way, in the room, on the shore, on the hill-side. Now He is recognised at once, now slowly and with growing conviction. But with every variety of circumstance there is one effect. The natural impression is—not to go further now—that the revelation was given according to the need and the power of those who received it; and hence we are encouraged to conclude that by this means the record corresponds with the needs and powers of all Christians to the end of time. As the revelation was a discipline and preparation then, so the record is a discipline and preparation now. The record is fragmentary, but it is also divinely typical. That which is incomplete as a history is complete as a Gospel.

2. If we now turn to the Revelation itself, two characteristics will at once strike us. It is a revelation of new modes of human life: it is a revelation made only to believers. It is not the exhibition of the continuance of an existence with which we are already acquainted, but the indication of an existence for which we look. It is for the Church and not for the world, to strengthen not to overpower.

INTRODUCTORY.

The Revelation of the Risen Christ is indeed, in the fullest sense of the word, a Revelation; an unveiling of that which was before undiscovered and unknown.

Nothing perhaps (if we may anticipate results yet to be established) is more surprising in the whole sum of inspired teaching than the way in which the different appearances of Christ after His Resurrection meet and satisfy the aspirations of man towards a knowledge of the unseen world. As we fix our thoughts steadily upon them we learn how our life is independent of its present conditions; how we also can live through death; how we can retain all the issues of the past without being bound by the limitations under which they were shaped. Christ rose from the grave changed and yet the same; and in Him we have the pledge and the type of our rising.

Christ was changed. He was no longer subject to the laws of the material order to which His earthly life was previously conformed. As has been well said: "What was natural to Him before is now miraculous; what was before miraculous is now natural." Or to put the thought in another form, in our earthly life the spirit is manifested through the body; in the life of the Risen Christ the Body is manifested (may we not say so?) through the Spirit. He "appears" and no longer is seen coming. He is found present, no one knows from whence; He passes away, no one knows whither. He stands in the midst of the group of Apostles *when the doors were shut for fear of the Jews. He vanishes out of the sight* of the disciples whose eyes were opened that they should know Him. And at last *as they were looking He was taken up, and a cloud received Him out of their sight.*

The continuity, the intimacy, the simple familiarity of former intercourse is gone. He is seen and recognised only as He wills, and when He wills. In the former sense of the phrase, He is no longer with the disciples. They have, it appears, no longer a natural power of recognising Him. Feeling and thought require to be purified and enlightened in order that He may be known under the conditions of earthly life. There is a mysterious awfulness about His Person which first inspires fear and then claims adoration. He appointed a place of meeting with His Apostles, but He did not accompany them on their journey. He belongs already to another realm, so that the Ascension only ratifies and presents in a final form the lessons of the forty days, in which it was included.

Thus Christ is seen to be changed, but none the less He is also seen to be essentially the same. Nothing has been left in the grave though all has been transfigured. He is the same, so that the marks of the Passion can become sensibly present to the doubting Thomas: the same, so that He can eat of the broiled fish which the disciples had prepared: the same, so that one word spoken with the old accent makes Him known to the weeping Magdalene: the same, so that above all expectation and against the evidence of death, the Apostles could proclaim to the world that He who suffered upon the Cross had indeed redeemed Israel; the same in patience, in tenderness, in chastening reproof, in watchful sympathy, in quickening love. In each narrative the marvellous contrast is written—Christ changed and yet the same—without effort, without premeditation, without consciousness, as it appears, on the part of the Evangelists. And if we put together these two series of facts in which the

INTRODUC- contrast is presented, we shall see how they
TORY. ennoble and complete our prospect of the future.
It is not that Christ's soul lives on divested of
the essence as of the accidents of the earthly
garments in which it was for a time arrayed. It
is not that His body, torn and wounded, is
restored, such as it was, to its former vigour and
beauty. But in Him soul and body, in the in-
dissoluble union of a perfect manhood, are seen
triumphant over the last penalty of sin. In Him
1 Cor. xv. first *the corruptible puts on incorruption, and the
53. mortal puts on immortality*, without ceasing to
'be,' so far as it has been, that in Him we
may learn something more of the possibilities of
human life, which, as far as we can observe it
with our present powers, is sad and fleeting;
that in Him we may lift our eyes to heaven our
home and find it about us even here; that in
Him we may be enabled to gain some sure confidence of fellowship with the departed; that in
Him we may have our hope steadfast, unmove-
able, knowing that our labour cannot be in vain.

Now if this be so, if the Lord after His
Resurrection laid open to men, as they could
bear it, a *new* life, it will be evident upon reflection that this knowledge could only be given to
Acts x. 41. the faithful: *God gave Him to be made manifest
not to all the people but unto witnesses that were*

chosen before by God. The Revelation was a Revelation to believers. This is the second characteristic which we have marked. If we compare the scenes of the Passion with the scenes of the Resurrection, we shall realise the significance of the contrast. If we compare the teaching of the Life of humiliation with the teaching of the Life of glory we shall realise its Divine necessity. That which is of the earth can perceive only that which is of the earth. Our senses can only grasp that which is kindred to themselves. We see no more than that for which we have a trained faculty of seeing. If then the Life of the Risen Lord had been simply a renovation or a continuance of His former life, subject to the same conditions, and necessarily destined to the same inevitable close, then the experience of unbelievers would have been sufficient to test, the witness of unbelievers would have been adequate to establish the reality of the Resurrection. But if it was a foreshadowing of new powers of human action, of a new mode of human being, then without a corresponding power of spiritual discernment there could be no testimony to its truth. The world could not see Christ, and Christ could not—there is a Divine impossibility—shew Himself to the world. To have proved by incontestable evidence that Christ rose again as

Mark vi. 5.

INTRODUC-TORY. Lazarus rose again, would have been not to confirm our faith, but to destroy it irretrievably. Only the believer, who, however imperfectly, yet vitally had felt Christ's power and known Him, could grasp and harmonise the two modes of the Revelation of His Person. On the eve of His Passion He had Himself shewn the condition John xiv. of this future knowledge. *Lord, what is come to* 22. *pass,* said one, *that thou wilt manifest Thyself to us and not unto the world?* and the answer was given for all time: *If a man love me......my Father will love him, and we will come unto him.*

The answer was given for all time. The law which held in the Apostolic age holds still. The revelation of the Risen Christ, the revelation of that life which shall be, is of necessity a revelation to believers. Sympathy is the imperative condition of apprehending the Divine Presence. The knowledge of Him who is perfect God and perfect man, the conqueror of death, the unfailing Advocate, is reserved for those who love Him and strive to attain to His likeness.

Yet a little while and the world beholdeth me no more; but ye behold me: because I live, ye shall live also.

I.

THE REVELATION THROUGH LOVE.

Ἀπῆλθον οὖν πάλιν πρὸς αὐτοὺς οἱ μαθηταί. Μαρία δὲ ἱστήκει πρὸς τῷ μνημείῳ ἔξω κλαίουσα. ὡς οὖν ἔκλαιεν παρέκυψεν εἰς τὸ μνημεῖον, καὶ θεωρεῖ δύο ἀγγέλους ἐν λευκοῖς καθεζομένους, ἕνα πρὸς τῇ κεφαλῇ καὶ ἕνα πρὸς τοῖς ποσίν, ὅπου ἔκειτο τὸ σῶμα τοῦ Ἰησοῦ. καὶ λέγουσιν αὐτῇ ἐκεῖνοι Γύναι, τί κλαίεις; λέγει αὐτοῖς ὅτι Ἦραν τὸν κύριόν μου, καὶ οὐκ οἶδα ποῦ ἔθηκαν αὐτόν. ταῦτα εἰποῦσα ἐστράφη εἰς τὰ ὀπίσω, καὶ θεωρεῖ τὸν Ἰησοῦν ἑστῶτα, καὶ οὐκ ᾔδει ὅτι Ἰησοῦς ἐστίν. λέγει αὐτῇ Ἰησοῦς Γύναι, τί κλαίεις; τίνα ζητεῖς; ἐκείνη δοκοῦσα ὅτι ὁ κηπουρός ἐστιν λέγει αὐτῷ Κύριε, εἰ σὺ ἐβάστασας αὐτόν, εἰπέ μοι ποῦ ἔθηκας αὐτόν, κἀγὼ αὐτὸν ἀρῶ. λέγει αὐτῇ Ἰησοῦς Μαριάμ. στραφεῖσα ἐκείνη λέγει αὐτῷ Ἑβραϊστί Ῥαββουνεί (ὃ λέγεται Διδάσκαλε). λέγει αὐτῇ Ἰησοῦς Μή μου ἅπτου, οὔπω γὰρ ἀναβέβηκα πρὸς τὸν πατέρα· πορεύου δὲ πρὸς τοὺς ἀδελφούς μου καὶ εἰπὲ αὐτοῖς Ἀναβαίνω πρὸς τὸν πατέρα μου καὶ πατέρα ὑμῶν καὶ θεόν μου καὶ θεὸν ὑμῶν. ἔρχεται Μαριὰμ ἡ Μαγδαληνὴ ἀγγέλλουσα τοῖς μαθηταῖς ὅτι Ἑώρακα τὸν κύριον καὶ ταῦτα εἶπεν αὐτῇ.

Ἀναστὰς δὲ πρωὶ πρώτῃ σαββάτου ἐφάνη πρῶτον Μαρίᾳ τῇ Μαγδαληνῇ, παρ' ἧς ἐκβεβλήκει ἑπτὰ δαιμόνια. ἐκείνη πορευθεῖσα ἀπήγγειλεν τοῖς μετ' αὐτοῦ γενομένοις πενθοῦσι καὶ κλαίουσιν· κἀκεῖνοι ἀκούσαντες ὅτι ζῇ καὶ ἐθεάθη ὑπ' αὐτῆς ἠπίστησαν.

So the disciples went away again unto their own home. But Mary was standing without at the tomb weeping: so, as she wept, she stooped and looked into the tomb; and she beholdeth two angels in white sitting, one at the head, and one at the feet, where the body of Jesus had lain. And they say unto her, Woman, why weepest thou? She saith unto them, They have taken away my Lord, and I know not where they have laid him. When she had thus said, she turned herself back, and beholdeth Jesus standing, and knew not that it was Jesus. Jesus saith unto her, Woman, why weepest thou? whom seekest thou? She, supposing him to be the gardener, saith unto him, Sir, if thou hast borne him hence, tell me where thou hast laid him, and I will take him away. Jesus saith unto her, Mary. She turneth herself, and saith unto him in Hebrew, Rabboni; which is to say, Master. Jesus saith to her, Touch me not; for I am not yet ascended unto the Father: but go unto my brethren, and say to them, I ascend unto my Father and your Father and my God and your God. Mary Magdalene cometh and telleth the disciples, I have seen the Lord; and how that he had said these things unto her.

JOHN xx. 10—18.

Now when he was risen early on the first day of the week, he appeared first to Mary Magdalene, from whom he had cast out seven devils. She went and told them that had been with him, as they mourned and wept. And they, when they heard that he was alive, and had been seen of her, disbelieved.

[MARK] xvi. 9—11.

Ὁ δὲ ἀγαπῶν με ἀγαπηθήσεται ὑπὸ τοῦ πατρός μου, κἀγὼ ἀγαπήσω αὐτὸν καὶ ἐμφανίσω αὐτῷ ἐμαυτόν.

He that loveth me shall be loved of my Father, and I will love him, and will manifest myself unto him.

JOHN xiv. 21.

THE REVELATION THROUGH LOVE.

WE have seen in a summary review that the record of the appearances of the Risen Lord is fragmentary and yet divinely significant: that the revelation which it contains of One changed and yet the same enables us to realise, so far as it is needful or possible for us to do so, new forms of human existence, and to pass in faith to the realm of being beyond the grave. As a Revelation the incidents preserved in our Gospels are complete: as a history they are most imperfect. The former truth will, as I trust, be established by the fuller examination of them which we have to make. The latter truth I simply restate with the object of cautioning those who study the Gospels for themselves against the perilous assumption that we are in possession of all the circumstances of the several events, so that we are bound either to arrange them in a harmonious whole or to confess that differences which we cannot completely reconcile must be fatal to the accuracy of the Evangelists. Much, I believe, will always remain uncertain; and the truest wisdom, the truest reverence, is to admit the difficulties which thus remain, sure of this that a fuller knowledge if it had been given us would have removed them.

We have already spoken of the general character of the manifestations of the Risen Christ. If we go a step farther we shall see that they fall both historically and spiritually into two groups, those of the first Easter Day and those of the days which followed. The appearances on Easter Day seem to be mainly directed to the creation of an immediate present belief: those which took place afterwards to the establishment of a belief in Christ's future and abiding Presence. All alike in different ways lay open the reality and the power of the spiritual life. But at first the true personal Resurrection of Christ in the fulness of divine power is the one fact which is variously revealed to the loving, the desponding, the doubting. Then the permanent connexion between Christ and His disciples is unfolded in successive scenes. The teaching of the one group culminates in the words: *Handle me and see, for a spirit hath not flesh and bones as ye behold me having;* and *As the Father hath sent me even so send I you.*

The other in the words: *Go ye and make disciples of all the nations...and lo, I am with you all the days, even unto the end of the world.*   I.
Matt.
xxviii. 19 f

Bearing this distinction in mind we pass to the consideration of the separate revelations of the Risen Lord. And while there is much that is difficult to fix with precision in the recorded incidents of the first Easter Morning, the main features of the events stand out plainly in all the records. Women who had attended the Lord and wished to offer to Him the last ministry of love visited the sepulchre early on the first day of the week, and found the stone rolled away from its mouth and the sepulchre empty. They heard then the tidings of the Resurrection by an angelic message and bore the news to the disciples. So it was that love first sought the lost Lord; and in answer to love He also first revealed Himself. The brief summary which has been preserved at the end of St Mark's Gospel, gives the testimony of the early Church: Jesus *when He was risen early on the first day of the week appeared first to Mary Magdalene.* [Mark]xvi. 9. Thus we know that the narrative of St John, which lies now before us, contains the first manifestation, the first words, the first command, of the Risen Lord. In this light every detail gains a fresh interest; and there is indeed

20   The discipline of

hardly a word in the record which if we ponder it does not add to the power of the lesson.

The Apostles, St Peter and St John, who had been called to the sepulchre by Mary Magdalene, had returned to their own home. They had verified her strange tidings, and then they waited no longer. But Mary herself could not leave the spot. She thought only of what she apprehended as her loss; and stood there weeping. She did not venture to enter the sepulchre as the Apostles had done, but as she wept she took courage just to look in (παρέκυψεν). Even then the one object on which she could dwell was her Lord. The vision and the inquiry of angels were unable to surprise or to rouse her. In reply to their question she repeats with two slight but significant changes (*my Lord* for *the Lord*, *I know* for *we know*) the words which she had before addressed to the Apostles. She pays no further regard to their presence: she makes no petition for their help: *They have taken my Lord*, she replies shortly, *and I know not where they have laid Him*. It is as if this was the one burden of her thoughts. To all else she is blind and deaf. Half mechanically her grief found expression and then *she turned back*. She may have felt, as we often do feel without seeing, that some one had come near. *She turned back and beholdeth Jesus standing, and knew not that it was Jesus.* How indeed could she know? For her Jesus was the dead Body which she had seen laid in the grave, and which she had come to embalm. 'Her Lord' was just that which symbolised and recalled His intercourse with her in old time. She could look back, but she could not look forward. Even so, *Jesus saith unto her, Woman, why weepest thou? whom seekest thou?*

His first words are thus an echo of the words of the angel: an echo and something more; for He does not pause at their inquiry. He adds a clause which half interprets the mourner's sorrow, and the mourner's error. The question 'Why weepest thou?' is deepened, explained, invested with a power of sympathy by the further question: *Whom seekest thou?* Such sorrow, so the words imply, must be for a person and not for a thing: rightly understood for the living and not for the dead. And the words were not wholly without effect. Mary Magdalene no longer, as before, simply sets forth her loss: that, she feels, is understood: and so she implies in the question which follows that the supposed gardener had divined her secret. Starting from the sense of fellowship she is so far moved as to look for some relief to her suspense. She, who had made no request to the angels, makes a request to the stranger. *Sir, if thou*—if thou a friend—*hast borne Him hence tell me where thou hast laid Him, and I will take Him away.* There is no need of explaining who that 'He' is. There is no reckoning for the future. Love makes her strength appear sufficient for any effort. *I will take Him away.* I, a weak and lonely woman, will provide that our most sacred treasure shall hereafter be exposed to no risk. At this point we must suppose that a brief pause followed. Mary received no answer, and fell back to her former attitude of mourning. Simple human love had, as it seemed, done its uttermost and done its uttermost in vain. Then, in the crisis of her hopelessness, Jesus saith to her *Mary.* He *calleth her by name* as the Good Shepherd, and in that personal address He awakens her true self, as when before He had cast out from her seven demons. The blinding veil of a self-chosen grief is torn off. She feels at once what she is and what the Speaker is to her. Simply, decisively, in word and act she expresses her new-born faith, and turning once again saith to Him *in the Hebrew tongue*—in the language of sacred converse—*Rabboni*—my Master.

Word and act express her faith, and express it both in its strength and in its failure. She welcomes Him whom she had lost, but she welcomes no more. She has no loftier title for Him than that which past experience had made precious, Master, Teacher, applied here only to the Lord after His Resurrection. She substitutes, as we can see, a knowledge of His true humanity for a knowledge of His whole Person, Divine as well as human. She thinks that she can now enjoy His restored Presence as in time past. She assumes that the return to the old life exhausts the sum of her Master's victory over death. Just as she would have been content before if only she could have found the dead Body which she had come to anoint, that Body which she called her Lord, so now she would be content if she could retain Him, as she seemed to see Him, in a corruptible or mortal body.

Therefore in His reply Christ disciplines and raises her love. *Touch me not*, He says, or rather *Take not hold of me, for I am not yet ascended to the Father*. Do not, that is, cling to me, as though you could know me as I am through that which falls under the senses. Do not embrace that which is partial as though it were complete. For I am not yet ascended to the Father: I have not yet entered upon, or, as the idea may perhaps be better expressed, I have not yet revealed under the forms of time that perfect communion with God in heaven which will give more than you can yet understand. There was indeed something beyond the outward restoration to earth which had to be realised before that fellowship towards which Mary reached could be established as abiding. When the Ascension, the last triumph, was apprehended, then, and not till then, she would be able to enjoy uninterruptedly the intercourse which was as yet impossible. Christ had come back, not for one, but for many. Meanwhile therefore there was an office for her to fulfil. Her love did not lose its reward. As she had been the first to bear to the disciples the tidings of that which seemed to be her loss and theirs, so she was appointed to be the first to announce to them the coming and glorious change which crowned Christ's work and established theirs. *Go to my brethren*, He continued, *and say unto them, I ascend unto my Father and your Father, and my God and your God.*

In this one brief sentence the final relation of Christ to His people is determined, that relation which holds for us. The thought of the Resurrection as a mere outward fact is swallowed up in the thought of the Ascension, which is its spiritual interpretation. The message is not 'I have risen,' but 'I ascend': and not 'I shall ascend,' but 'I ascend.' The revelation was in part a promise as well as a fulfilment. The Lord's work was done; but its import had to be progressively apprehended by men. For Christ Himself the change from death to life, from humiliation to glory, was complete; but its fulness had to be made known to the Apostles. The ascent to the Father was the condition of the greater works which they were to do. Accordingly the transformation which was at last symbolised by the visible taking up into heaven was being brought home to them during the forty days, as they gradually became familiarised with the nature of their Master's higher life. And as Christ binds His followers to Himself in this His first greeting of victory, so at the same time He makes clear for ever the difference of being by which He is separated from them. They are 'brethren,' sons with Him of one Father, but sons otherwise than He is: they by adoption, He by essence: they in Him, He in Himself. Their Father is His Father, their God is His God, yet in different relations. The words sound to us from that first Easter message harmonising the contrasts and conflicts of our divided being, proclaiming earth to be heaven's ante-chamber, uniting without confounding the Divine and human. *I ascend*, Christ says, not to our Father, as if one term could embrace Him and His, not to my Father alone, not to your Father alone, but—*to my Father and your Father, and my God and your God.*

[margin: I.]
[margin: John xiv. 12.]
[margin: John xx. 17.]

26   *The present importance*

I.

John xiv. 21.

Such appear to be the stages in this first manifestation of the Risen Christ, in which He fulfilled His promise, 'I will manifest myself to him that loveth me.' It was through the love of the weak that the Resurrection was announced to the Apostles. We can at once acknowledge the fitness of the divine order; and if we observe in the unfolding of the marvellous history the blindness of self-concentrated sorrow, the haste, I had almost said, the wilfulness of love, and on the other hand the tenderness of Christ's personal voice, His disciplining of mistaken devotion, His raising of imperfect faith, His injunction of an Evangelic charge, we shall see how we have in it a clear exhibition of the significance of the Resurrection as a beginning, a preparation, a pledge of our fellowship even now with a spiritual order, to which we are trained to strive forward, and which we are bound, according to our powers, to seek and to shew about us. We shall see how we have in it lessons which can never be out of date, a manifestation luminous for our own days.

[Mark] xvi. 9.

Not on the first Easter Morning only have those who have truly loved Christ, those who have felt His healing power, those who have offered up all to His service, been tempted to substitute the dead Body for the living Lord: not on the first

Easter Morning only have devout and passionate worshippers sought to make that which is of the earth the centre and the type of their service: not on the first Easter Morning only have believers been inclined to claim absolute permanence for their own partial apprehension of Truth: not on the first Easter Morning only, but in this later age I will venture to say more than then. For it is impossible when we look at the subjects and methods of current controversy not to ask ourselves sadly whether we ourselves are busy in building the tomb of Christ, or really ready to recognise Him if He comes to us in the form of a new life; whether we are fruitlessly mourning over a loss which is, in fact, the condition of a blessing, or waiting trustfully for the transfigurement of the dead past. It is impossible to open many popular books of devotion, or to read many modern hymns, without feeling that materialism has invaded faith no less than science, and that enervating sentimentalism is corrupting the fresh springs of manly and simple service. It is impossible not to fear, when in the widespread searching of hearts men cling almost desperately to traditional phrases and customs, that we may forget the call of Christ to occupy new regions of thought and labour in His Name.

The dangers are indeed most pressing, but the

I. narrative on which we have just dwelt, while it reveals their essential character brings to us hope in facing them. If the love, in virtue of which alone they are formidable, narrow, misguided, intolerant, as it is, is also sincere, it cannot finally miss its true object. The love of Mary which at first hid Christ, none the less brought her to Him and Him to her. He appeared to her first, as we must believe, because she was most conscious of her need of Him. He in due time interpreted her need though she misunderstood it. She saw no more than she expected to see, but He opened her eyes to a truer vision. He made Himself known through sympathy. Such is the law of His working. His earliest words to every suffering child of man will always be 'Why weepest thou? Whom seekest thou?' The sorrow which partly veils the Presence quickens the search. And if the voice, when it comes to each one of us, awakens in the silence of our souls the true conviction that we do want a living Friend and Saviour and not a dead Body, some relic which we can decorate with our offerings or some formula which we can repeat with easy pertinacity, then we in our turn shall be strengthened to bear the discipline by which Christ in His glory leads us to a fuller and truer view of Himself and of His kingdom. We shall endure gladly the removal of that which for the time would only minister to error: we shall be privileged to announce to others that He whom we have found through tears and left in patient obedience, is moving onwards to loftier scenes of triumph: we shall learn to understand why the Lord's own message of His Resurrection was not 'I have risen' or 'I live,' but 'I ascend:' we shall listen till all experience and all history, all that is in the earth of good and beautiful and true, grows articulate with one command, the familiar words of our common service, *Sursum corda,* 'Lift up your hearts;' and we shall answer in humble devotion, in patient faith, in daily struggles within and without, 'We lift them up unto the Lord,' to the Lord Risen and Ascended.

APPENDIX TO I.

Καὶ ἀπελθοῦσαι ταχὺ ἀπὸ τοῦ μνημείου μετὰ φόβου καὶ χαρᾶς μεγάλης ἔδραμον ἀπαγγεῖλαι τοῖς μαθηταῖς αὐτοῦ. καὶ ἰδοὺ Ἰησοῦς ὑπήντησεν αὐταῖς λέγων Χαίρετε· αἱ δὲ προσελθοῦσαι ἐκράτησαν αὐτοῦ τοὺς πόδας καὶ προσεκύνησαν αὐτῷ. τότε λέγει αὐταῖς ὁ Ἰησοῦς Μὴ φοβεῖσθε· ὑπάγετε ἀπαγγείλατε τοῖς ἀδελφοῖς μου ἵνα ἀπέλθωσιν εἰς τὴν Γαλιλαίαν, κἀκεῖ με ὄψονται.

And they departed quickly from the tomb with fear and great joy, and ran to bring his disciples word. And behold, Jesus met them, saying, All hail. And they came and took hold of his feet, and worshipped him. Then saith Jesus unto them, Fear not: go tell my brethren that they depart into Galilee, and there shall they see me.
MATT. xxviii. 8—10.

I.

IT is difficult to determine the relation in which this narrative stands to John xx. 10—18. It has been held that St Matthew, giving a summary account of the manifestations of the Lord, has described the appearance to Mary Magdalene as given to the women generally, of whom Mary was the representative. Others again have maintained that the appearance to 'the women' was distinct from the appearance to Mary Magdalene, and granted to them on their way from the sepulchre while Mary still lingered there. In support of the first view it is urged that the narratives of St Matthew and St John, while they differ in details, agree in the most important features. In both cases homage is offered to the Lord in the same way (Matt. xxviii. 9; John xx. 17): in both cases He abruptly cuts it short by enjoining the deliverance of a message to the Apostles: in both cases He calls the Apostles by the unique title of 'brethren' (Matt. xxviii. 10; John xx. 17).

On the other hand it may be replied that such coincidences correspond with the similarity of circumstances: that the feelings of the women would be in a great degree like the feelings of Mary, and so would be disciplined by the Lord in the like manner: that there is no improbability in two such revelations: that this being so, it is more reasonable to maintain the full natural sense of the two narratives, which implies two incidents.

It is not material to our present purpose to choose between these two different views. The narrative of St Matthew adds nothing to that of St John in respect to the appearance of the Lord as a revelation of Himself. The general phrases 'All hail' (Χαίρετε, v. 9), and 'Fear not' (v. 10), have a more emphatic expression in the personal addresses 'Woman, why weepest thou?' (John xx. 15), and 'Mary' (John xx. 16). So also the connexion of the vision of the Lord with Galilee, suggests the idea which is presented in its most complete form in the announcement of the Lord's Ascension in St John.

The corresponding details which have been preserved in the two narratives must be taken together. When so studied the message recorded by St John throws light upon that recorded by St Matthew. In this connexion it cannot but seem strange that many writers should have supposed that the command, *Go tell my brethren that they depart into Galilee, and there shall they see me* (Matt. xxviii. 10), excludes the idea of manifestations of the Lord at Jerusalem. It would be equally just to argue that the message in St John, *Go unto my brethren and say to them I ascend unto my Father*... (John xx. 17), excludes all further manifestations whatsoever. In each case a decisive truth was indicated.

and to Mary Magdalene.

Jerusalem was set aside from being the spiritual centre of the new kingdom (comp. Matt. iv. 15 f.), though the disciples tarried there that all the teaching of the Law might find fulfilment (Luke xxiv. 48 f.). So it was that Christ was revealed in Galilee as the universal sovereign, although the disciples started from Jerusalem on the fulfilment of their world-wide mission (Acts i. 8). And again Christ was to be proclaimed in His Divine exaltation: His return to the Father was the condition of the greater works which the disciples were to accomplish. Thus the vision in Galilee and the ascent to the Father served to characterise the revelation which was to be given.

It is worthy of notice that the Hebrew (Nazarene) Gospel recorded (so far as there is direct information) only appearances of the Lord at Jerusalem, to James (comp. 1 Cor. xv. 7), and 'to those with Peter' (Luke xxiv. 36 ff.).

II.

THE REVELATION THROUGH THOUGHT.

Καὶ ἰδοὺ δύο ἐξ αὐτῶν ἐν αὐτῇ τῇ ἡμέρᾳ ἦσαν πορευόμενοι εἰς κώμην ἀπέχουσαν σταδίους ἑξήκοντα ἀπὸ Ἰερουσαλήμ, ᾗ ὄνομα Ἐμμαούς καὶ αὐτοὶ ὡμίλουν πρὸς ἀλλήλους περὶ πάντων τῶν συμβεβηκότων τούτων. καὶ ἐγένετο ἐν τῷ ὁμιλεῖν αὐτοὺς καὶ συνζητεῖν [καὶ] αὐτὸς Ἰησοῦς ἐγγίσας συνεπορεύετο αὐτοῖς, οἱ δὲ ὀφθαλμοὶ αὐτῶν ἐκρατοῦντο τοῦ μὴ ἐπιγνῶναι αὐτόν. εἶπεν δὲ πρὸς αὐτούς Τίνες οἱ λόγοι οὗτοι οὓς ἀντιβάλλετε πρὸς ἀλλήλους περιπατοῦντες; καὶ ἐστάθησαν σκυθρωποί. ἀποκριθεὶς δὲ εἷς ὀνόματι Κλεόπας εἶπεν πρὸς αὐτόν Σὺ μόνος παροικεῖς Ἰερουσαλὴμ καὶ οὐκ ἔγνως τὰ γενόμενα ἐν αὐτῇ ἐν ταῖς ἡμέραις ταύταις; καὶ εἶπεν αὐτοῖς Ποῖα; οἱ δὲ εἶπαν αὐτῷ Τὰ περὶ Ἰησοῦ τοῦ Ναζαρηνοῦ, ὃς ἐγένετο ἀνὴρ προφήτης δυνατὸς ἐν ἔργῳ καὶ λόγῳ ἐναντίον τοῦ θεοῦ καὶ παντὸς τοῦ λαοῦ, ὅπως τε παρέδωκαν αὐτὸν οἱ ἀρχιερεῖς καὶ οἱ ἄρχοντες ἡμῶν εἰς κρίμα θανάτου καὶ ἐσταύρωσαν αὐτόν. ἡμεῖς δὲ ἠλπίζομεν ὅτι αὐτός ἐστιν ὁ μέλλων λυτροῦσθαι τὸν Ἰσραήλ· ἀλλά γε καὶ σὺν πᾶσιν τούτοις τρίτην ταύτην ἡμέραν ἄγει ἀφ' οὗ ταῦτα ἐγένετο. ἀλλὰ καὶ γυναῖκές τινες ἐξ ἡμῶν ἐξέστησαν ἡμᾶς, γενόμεναι ὀρθριναὶ ἐπὶ τὸ μνημεῖον καὶ μὴ εὑροῦσαι τὸ σῶμα αὐτοῦ ἦλθαν λέγουσαι καὶ ὀπτασίαν ἀγγέλων ἑωρακέναι, οἳ λέγουσιν αὐτὸν ζῆν. καὶ ἀπῆλθάν τινες τῶν σὺν ἡμῖν ἐπὶ τὸ μνημεῖον, καὶ εὗρον οὕτως καθὼς αἱ γυναῖκες εἶπον, αὐτὸν δὲ οὐκ εἶδον. καὶ αὐτὸς εἶπεν πρὸς αὐτούς Ὦ ἀνόητοι καὶ βραδεῖς τῇ καρδίᾳ τοῦ πιστεύειν ἐπὶ πᾶσιν οἷς ἐλάλησαν οἱ προφῆται· οὐχὶ ταῦτα ἔδει παθεῖν τὸν χριστὸν καὶ

And behold, two of them were going that very day to a village named Emmaus, which was threescore furlongs from Jerusalem. And they communed with each other of all these things which had happened. And it came to pass, while they communed and questioned together, that Jesus himself drew near, and went with them. But their eyes were holden that they should not know him. And he said unto them, What communications are these that ye have one with another, as ye walk? And they stood still, looking sad. And one of them, named Cleopas, answering said unto him, Dost thou alone sojourn in Jerusalem and not know the things which are come to pass there in these days? And he said unto them, What things? And they said unto him, The things concerning Jesus of Nazareth, which was a prophet mighty in deed and word before God and all the people: and how the chief priests and our rulers delivered him up to be condemned to death, and crucified him. But we hoped that it was he which should redeem Israel. Yea and beside all this, it is now the third day since these things came to pass. Moreover certain women of our company amazed us, having been early at the tomb; and when they found not his body, they came, saying, that they had also seen a vision of angels, which said that he was alive. And certain of them that were with us went to the tomb, and found it even so as the women had said: but him they saw not. And he said unto them, O foolish men, and slow of heart to believe in all that the prophets have spoken! Behoved it not the Christ to suffer these things, and to enter into his glory? And beginning

εἰcελθεῖν εἰc τὴν Δόξαν αὐτοῦ; καὶ ἀρξάμενοc ἀπὸ
Μωυcέωc καὶ ἀπὸ πάντων τῶν προφητῶν Διερμή-
νευcεν αὐτοῖc ἐν πάcαιc ταῖc γραφαῖc τὰ περὶ ἑαυτοῦ.
Καὶ ἤγγιcαν εἰc τὴν κώμην οὗ ἐπορεύοντο, καὶ αὐτὸc
προcεποιήcατο πορρώτερον πορεύεcθαι. καὶ παρε-
βιάcαντο αὐτὸν λέγοντεc Μεῖνον μεθ᾽ ἡμῶν, ὅτι πρὸc
ἑcπέραν ἐcτὶν καὶ κέκλικεν ἤδη ἡ ἡμέρα. καὶ εἰc-
ῆλθεν τοῦ μεῖναι cὺν αὐτοῖc. Καὶ ἐγένετο ἐν τῷ
κατακλιθῆναι αὐτὸν μετ᾽ αὐτῶν λαβὼν τὸν ἄρτον
εὐλόγηcεν καὶ κλάcαc ἐπεδίδου αὐτοῖc· αὐτῶν δὲ
Διηνοίχθηcαν οἱ ὀφθαλμοὶ καὶ ἐπέγνωcαν αὐτόν· καὶ
αὐτὸc ἄφαντοc ἐγένετο ἀπ᾽ αὐτῶν. καὶ εἶπαν πρὸc
ἀλλήλουc Οὐχὶ ἡ καρδία ἡμῶν καιομένη ἦν ὡc
ἐλάλει ἡμῖν ἐν τῇ ὁδῷ ὡc διήνοιγεν ἡμῖν τὰc γρα-
φάc; Καὶ ἀναcτάντεc αὐτῇ τῇ ὥρᾳ ὑπέcτρεψαν εἰc
Ἰερουcαλήμ, καὶ εὗρον ἠθροιcμένουc τοὺc ἕνδεκα καὶ
τοὺc cὺν αὐτοῖc, λέγονταc ὅτι ὄντωc ἠγέρθη ὁ κύριοc
καὶ ὤφθη Σίμωνι. καὶ αὐτοὶ ἐξηγοῦντο τὰ ἐν τῇ
ὁδῷ καὶ ὡc ἐγνώcθη αὐτοῖc ἐν τῇ κλάcει τοῦ ἄρτου.

Μετὰ δὲ ταῦτα δυcὶν ἐξ αὐτῶν περιπατοῦcιν
ἐφανερώθη ἐν ἑτέρᾳ μορφῇ πορευομένοιc εἰc ἀγρόν·
κἀκεῖνοι ἀπελθόντεc ἀπήγγειλαν τοῖc λοιποῖc· οὐδὲ
ἐκείνοιc ἐπίcτευcαν.

from Moses and from all the prophets, he interpreted to them in all the scriptures the things concerning himself. And they drew nigh unto the village, whither they were going: and he made as though he would go further. And they constrained him, saying, Abide with us: for it is toward evening, and the day is now far spent. And he went in to abide with them. And it came to pass, when he had sat down with them to meat, he took the bread, and blessed it, and brake, and gave to them. And their eyes were opened, and they knew him; and he vanished out of their sight. And they said one to another, Was not our heart burning within us, while he spake to us in the way, while he opened to us the scriptures? And they rose up that very hour, and returned to Jerusalem, and found the eleven gathered together, and them that were with them, saying, The Lord is risen indeed, and hath appeared to Simon. And they rehearsed the things that happened in the way, and how he was known of them in the breaking of the bread.

LUKE xxiv. 13—35.

And after these things he was manifested in another form unto two of them, as they walked, on their way into the country. And they went away and told it unto the rest: neither believed they them.

[MARK] xvi. 12 f.

Ἐγήγερται τῇ ἡμέρᾳ τῇ τρίτῃ κατὰ τὰς γραφάς.

He hath been raised on the third day according to the scriptures.

1 COR. xv. 4.

THE REVELATION THROUGH THOUGHT.

THERE are two ways, it may be said generally, by which we can attain the highest spiritual truth, the way of feeling, and the way of thought. The heart stirred by religious affection knows its own wants and directly recognises Him who can satisfy them. The understanding quickened by a sense of Divine order in life comes to acknowledge Him in Whom the promise of the ages is fulfilled. So it was that on the first Easter Day the Risen Lord revealed Himself to Mary Magdalene and afterwards to the two disciples on the way to Emmaus, and through their contrasted experience prepared the disciples for the crowning revelation to the assembled body. He purified feeling and He disciplined thought, that His great commission might be welcomed and accomplished.

The manifestation to the two disciples is closely related as a parallel, a contrast and a complement to the manifestation to Mary Magdalene. Both were appearances to individual disciples; both were appearances to those who were sadly mourning over a supposed loss; both were for a time

II.

Luke xxiv. 13 ff.

misinterpreted; both were at last apprehended as laying open hitherto unknown spheres of Truth. So far they were alike, but in other respects they were widely different. That first appearance was granted to a loving woman, this to reasoning men: that was the elevation of personal devotion, this was the confirmation of social hope: that discloses to us something of the conditions of Christ's Presence, this discloses to us something of the manner in which the Presence is offered and realised.

Thus the two revelations have remarkable features of likeness and difference; and when taken together the two signally illustrate the principle which has been laid down that the Evangelic records, however fragmentary (not contradictory) as a history, are complete as a revelation. They cover a large part of the separate experience of Christians. We can find in them each for ourselves the divine answer to our own characteristic difficulties, the sufficient pledges to assure us that Christ is waiting to help us; that He is ready on the one side to lift our affections to a loftier realm than we have yet reached, and on the other to guide our reasonings to surer conclusions than we have yet gained.

The first thing perhaps which strikes us in the history of the appearance to the two disciples as a history, is the fact that we know nothing more

The two disciples unknown.

of the disciples themselves than what the incident itself brings to notice. They were not Apostles; they were not (so far as it appears) in any way distinguished. In this respect they were unlike Mary Magdalene, whose personality brings out the inmost character of the lesson which she received. Feeling indeed is in its essence personal, while thought is in its essence impersonal. Of one of the disciples the name has been preserved; but of him we possess no more individual details; and the name Cleopas, though similar in sound to that of Clopas (Cleophas), the father of James, is wholly distinct from it. Of the other nothing can even be conjectured with any probability. They appear, if I may so speak, as average men from the company of the first believers. For a brief space they stand in the full light of the Divine Presence; they shew their expectations, their difficulties, their weakness, their strength; they deliver their witness and then they are lost in the church. They are lost, and at the same time the lesson which they had first been allowed to learn shaped the Apostolic interpretation of the Old Testament.

II.

John xix. 25; Matt. x. 3.

But though these two disciples are themselves unknown, nothing can be more vivid or more natural than the picture which is drawn of the conflict of their thoughts. They had heard the first tidings of the Easter Morning, of the vision of angels and of the empty tomb. But these vague and uncertain messages seemed to them wholly outweighed by the terrible and patent fact of the Crucifixion. Such reports, partially confirmed by some of the Apostolic company, were not even sufficient to keep them in Jerusalem till something more definite could be ascertained. They had once looked for a national deliverance. They had once hoped that Jesus of Nazareth was the promised Saviour: *He that should redeem Israel.* But that expectation was over. His death, so they concluded, had falsified their former belief. And even His Personal appearance to them, as they were then minded, would not have restored what seemed to have been taken away. But while this was so, they still clung loyally to so much of their original faith as was untouched by the tragic end of their Master. Like Mary, though in another sense, they held the dead Christ to be their Lord. They were not ashamed to reckon themselves still followers of the Crucified. They ventured to proclaim even to a stranger that He who had so died was a mighty prophet. They assumed that His fate was the one chief subject of attention. *Dost thou alone sojourn in Jerusalem,* they said to their questioner, *and not know the things which are come to pass there in these days?* They still felt that the surprising rumours of the women, coupled with what their Lord had said more than once of a vision on *the third day*, might have some meaning which they had not at present learnt. Their debate was eager and earnest. But as yet their interpretation of the past barred the way to the fulness of faith.

Such was their position, *when it came to pass that while they communed and questioned together Jesus Himself drew near and went with them.* And since it was so, it was no marvel that their *eyes were holden that they should not know Him.* We need not speculate as to the manner in which *their eyes were holden.* It is enough for us to remember that God may rightly be said to do through His inexorable laws that which we ourselves bring about. We can see (as I said before) only that which we have the faculty of seeing. And if we fail to train, to use, to refine our power of vision, so far our eyes are holden. The want of outward perception may in this case have corresponded with the want of inward perception. The disciples loved still and Christ came: they doubted and His person was veiled. He came that He might be known, yet He could only be known by the faith which He purposed to quicken. There was a hiding, so to speak, without that there might be a manifestation within. The fact is a speaking parable.

II.   But though the disciples failed to recognise their fellow-traveller, they were at once arrested by His questions. Currents of sympathy were mingled with this first address as when He spoke to Mary: *They stood still, looking sad,* and in reply they laid bare their hearts. This indeed was Christ's design. It was not that they could tell Him anything which He did not know, but rather He enabled them to give distinct shape to their own sorrows.

Then when all was set forth up to the last pathetic utterance, *but Him they saw not,* the Lord at once met the doubts which they had raised and to which they had yielded. With loving decisiveness he marked sharply their double error: *O foolish men and slow of heart to believe in all that the prophets have spoken.* They had failed to believe the prophets from lack of intelligence and from lack of sympathy. They were without the mental force which seizes the whole scope of the divine order: they were without the moral enthusiasm which reconciles seeming contradictions. He led them therefore as they could follow to a fuller view of God's ways. He helped them to see that their central difficulty—the Crucifixion of Jesus—was in fact an essential part of the counsel of God. So far from it being true, as they had thought, that suffering was fatal to

Luke xxiv. 25.

the Messiahship of Jesus of Nazareth, their new companion made them feel that it was necessary *that the Christ should suffer and so enter into His glory. And beginning from Moses, and from all the prophets, He interpreted to them in all the Scriptures the things concerning Himself.*

It is easy to understand how the great truth, 'Redemption through Sacrifice,' dawned upon them as He spoke: how they welcomed the reproof which opened the way to truer knowledge: how their hearts were kindled with a fire of love: how the whole course of their national history became luminous with a purpose which they saw fulfilled in their crucified Master. The hope which was quenched came back. The faint spark of remaining faith was fanned into a flame. Then came the end. Christ had joined them of His good pleasure; they kept Him, when He offered them the choice of separation, of their own will. It was indeed natural that they should constrain such a Teacher to abide with them. It was natural that He should take the chief place at their evening meal. By this time their souls were in sympathy with His whole life and work. And so *it came to pass when He had sat down with them to meat, He took the bread and blessed and brake and gave to them; and their eyes were opened and they knew Him.* A moment was sufficient for the

50 *The lesson of*

II. full and final apprehension of the crowning Truth. For an instant they saw in glory what they had at length felt to be Divine even in humiliation, and then *He vanished out of their sight.*

Such is the history; and the manifestation had done its work. There was no need of any longer continuance of the Lord's visible Presence. Just as Mary had been forbidden to cling to Him whom she had recovered, so for these two disciples it was *expedient that* the Lord *should go away.* He was parted from them for a season that they might have Him for ever. But like Mary they learnt that their experience was not for themselves alone. Without any express command faith interpreted its mission: *They rose up that very hour and returned to Jerusalem...And they rehearsed the things that happened in the way and how* [*the Lord*] *was known of them in the breaking of the bread.*

If now we endeavour to gather into a brief compass the abiding lesson of this second recorded appearance of the Risen Christ, we may, I think, say truly that it conveys to us a lively sense of the way in which the Lord is the life of all history. Not in startling visitations or great deliverances only, but in the still, gentle, currents of life He is working His good pleasure. Not in

the manifestation. 51

a few scattered predictions, but in all the Scriptures we find *the things concerning Him*. Far beneath the outward sign—the type, the judgment, the word—lies *the spirit of prophecy* which is *the witness to Jesus*. Above all it shews to us how the great mystery of suffering and death is the condition for the conquest of evil and not the declaration of the triumph of evil. *If it behoved*, if, that is, it was in accordance with the will of God, *that the Christ should suffer* and so *enter into His glory*, and if we can be enabled to see this necessity and see also the noble issues which flow from it, then we can understand how the same necessity must in due measure be laid upon His brethren. And those who have had the courage to look upon the whole state of the world and of humanity, who have watched the slow agonies of a last illness, who have felt the awful silence when the breath long feebly drawn comes no more, who have looked upon the cold marble features which hardly recall the loved form, will know that we need such light in the darkness of the inevitable future. It is most false, false to experience and false to the Gospel, to deny or to extenuate the reality and the bitterness of grief and pain. And it is not surprising that clear thinkers, who are deaf to the voice of the Risen Christ, maintain that this chequered world must have been made

[margin: 11.]
[margin: Rev. xix. 10.]

by a Being imperfect either in goodness or in power. But, thanks be to God, Christ has reconciled in His own Person the contradictions of life, and proved once for all that through these comes at last the perfect fulfilment of a Father's wisdom, and of a Father's love.

Under one aspect then, Christ, the Risen Christ, is everywhere present though our eyes be holden, and in Him all things are; but this history of the journey to Emmaus carries with it other and more personal teachings. It brings before us how Christ, the Risen Christ, in a special sense draws near to each one of us severally: how He adds Himself to the two or three gathered together in His name: how He journeys with us: how He enlightens our reason and fires our affections: how He abides under the shelter of our dwellings: how at some supreme moment, it may be, He allows us to see, with the eyes of the spirit, a brief vision of His majesty.

For that which was enacted on the evening of the first Lord's Day has been fulfilled, and is fulfilled no less surely and tenderly through the experience of all believers. Christ draws near to us now, as to those unknown wayfarers, with purposes of love.

Christ draws near to us when in the sacred intercourse of friendship we speak of our highest hopes and of our greatest sorrows, when we dare to throw off the veil of conventional irony, and talk openly of that which we know to lie deepest in our nature.

Christ draws near to us at the sad season when He seems to have been finally taken away, if we are not ashamed to confess, in the apparent disappointment of our hopes, that we are still His disciples.

Christ draws near to us when at some solemn appeal we pause on our journey, and stand in wondering sorrow perhaps, not knowing what answer to give to an unexpected and importunate questioner whose words touch us to the quick.

Christ draws near to us at the very crisis when we strive to give distinctness to our misgivings and to our difficulties. He asks us to speak freely to Him, and accepts the most imperfect confession of a sincere faith as the basis of His tender discipline.

Christ draws near to us when humbly and honestly we ponder His word. The study is difficult—far more difficult than we commonly suppose, and far more fruitful—but He illuminates the dark places, and through a better understanding of the letter guides us to a warmer sympathy with the spirit.

Christ draws near to us when we take gladly

the reproof which reveals to us our ignorance and our coldness, and resolutely strive to retain in our company the Teacher who by sharp methods has made us better able to see the Truth.

Christ draws near to us when we are bidden to draw near to Him at His Holy Table, and there gives us back with His blessing the offerings which we have brought to Him.

So Christ draws near to us, or at least He waits to draw near to us, in the manifold changes of our mortal life, near to us as we go in and go out in the fulfilment of our common duties, near to us when we are reassembled in our homes, near to us in the time of trial and in the hour of death.

The journey to Emmaus is indeed both in its apparent sadness and in its final joy an allegory of many a life. We traverse our appointed path with a sense of a void unfilled, of hopes unsatisfied, of promises withdrawn. The words of encouragement which come to us, often from strange sources, are not sufficient to bring back the assurance which we have lost. Yet happy are we if we open our griefs to Him who indeed knows them better than ourselves, if we keep Him by our side, if we constrain Him to abide with us. Happy if at the end, when the day is far spent, and darkness is closing round, we are allowed to see for one moment the fulness of the Divine Presence which has been with us all along half cloud and half light. But happier, and thrice happy, if when our hearts first burn within us, while life is still fresh and the way is still open, as One speaks to us in silent whisperings of reproof and discipline, speaks to us in the ever-living record of the Bible, we recognise the source of the spiritual fire. This we may do—nay, rather, if our faith be a reality, this we must do—and so feel that there has dawned upon us from the Easter Day a splendour over which no night can fall.

The Resurrection of Christ is no isolated fact. It is not only an answer to the craving of the human heart; it is the key to all history, the interpretation of the growing purpose of life: *Christ hath been raised*, not as some new, strange, unprepared thing, but *Christ hath been raised according to the Scriptures*. So God fulfilled the promises which in many parts and in many fashions lie written in the whole record of the Bible.

III.

THE CONVICTION OF FAITH.

Ταῦτα δὲ αὐτῶν λαλούντων αὐτὸς ἔστη ἐν μέσῳ αὐτῶν [καὶ λέγει αὐτοῖς Εἰρήνη ὑμῖν]. πτοηθέντες δὲ καὶ ἔμφοβοι γενόμενοι ἐδόκουν πνεῦμα θεωρεῖν. καὶ εἶπεν αὐτοῖς Τί τεταραγμένοι ἐστέ, καὶ διὰ τί διαλογισμοὶ ἀναβαίνουσιν ἐν τῇ καρδίᾳ ὑμῶν; ἴδετε τὰς χεῖράς μου καὶ τοὺς πόδας μου ὅτι ἐγώ εἰμι αὐτός· ψηλαφήσατέ με καὶ ἴδετε, ὅτι πνεῦμα σάρκα καὶ ὀστέα οὐκ ἔχει καθὼς ἐμὲ θεωρεῖτε ἔχοντα. [καὶ τοῦτο εἰπὼν ἔδειξεν αὐτοῖς τὰς χεῖρας καὶ τοὺς πόδας.] Ἔτι δὲ ἀπιστούντων αὐτῶν ἀπὸ τῆς χαρᾶς καὶ θαυμαζόντων εἶπεν αὐτοῖς Ἔχετέ τι βρώσιμον ἐνθάδε; οἱ δὲ ἐπέδωκαν αὐτῷ ἰχθύος ὀπτοῦ μέρος καὶ λαβὼν ἐνώπιον αὐτῶν ἔφαγεν.

Ὕστερον [δὲ] ἀνακειμένοις αὐτοῖς τοῖς ἕνδεκα ἐφανερώθη, καὶ ὠνείδισεν τὴν ἀπιστίαν αὐτῶν καὶ σκληροκαρδίαν ὅτι τοῖς θεασαμένοις αὐτὸν ἐγηγερμένον [ἐκ νεκρῶν] οὐκ ἐπίστευσαν.

And as they spake these things, he himself stood in the midst of them, and saith unto them, Peace be unto you. But they were terrified and affrighted, and supposed that they beheld a spirit. And he said unto them, Why are ye troubled? and wherefore do reasonings arise in your heart? See my hands and my feet, that it is I myself: handle me, and see; for a spirit hath not flesh and bones, as ye behold me having. [And when he had said this, he shewed them his hands and his feet.] And while they still disbelieved for joy, and wondered, he said unto them, Have ye here anything to eat? And they gave him a piece of broiled fish. And he took it, and did eat before them.

LUKE xxiv. 36—43.

And afterward he was manifested unto the eleven themselves as they sat at meat; and he upbraided them with their unbelief and hardness of heart, because they believed not them which had seen him after he was risen.

[MARK] xvi. 14.

Ἐγενόμην νεκρὸс καὶ ἰδοὺ ζῶν εἰμὶ εἰс τοὺс
αἰῶναс τῶν αἰώνων.

I was dead, and behold, I am alive for evermore.

Apoc. i. 18.

THE CONVICTION OF FAITH.

THE appearances of the Risen Lord which we have already considered, the appearance to Mary Magdalene, and the appearance to the two disciples on the road to Emmaus, were distinctively appearances to individuals, suited to meet personal needs and to satisfy personal misgivings. And there was still a third appearance of the same kind on the first Easter Day, of which the occurrence only has been recorded. When the wayfarers returned to Jerusalem *they found the eleven gathered together, and them that were with them, saying, The Lord is risen indeed and hath appeared to Simon.* We can imagine in some measure what that meeting with St Peter was: how the bitter tears of the Apostle were welcomed and stayed: how he was prepared for the fulfilment of the second part of his Master's words as the first had been sadly fulfilled : *Thou canst not follow me now ; but thou shalt follow afterwards :* how he was disciplined so as to keep only the courage out of his former confidence, and only

III.

Luke xxiv. 33 f.

John xiii. 36.

III.
Luke xxii.
31 ff.

the spirit of self-sacrifice out of his former impetuous devotion.

In these three personal appearances the Risen Lord dealt with the three greatest personal trials of men: with bereavement, with doubt, and with sin. He shewed that love will not ever in the end be left desolate or wasted. He shewed that patient thought will be guided at last through larger experience and fuller sympathy to sustaining truth. He shewed that penitence is effectual with God. But still something remained to be done before the day was ended. Christianity deals not only with individuals but with a society. The Gospel is embodied in a Church. It was necessary therefore, if we dare so speak, that the Risen Christ should reveal Himself to the representatives of His future Church, and make clear to them the completeness of His victory over death: that He should on the one hand shew them evidently the nature of their announcement; and that He should on the other confirm to them the authority of their commission. This was what He did when He presented Himself on the evening of the first Lord's Day to the little company, gathered together, as we cannot but believe, in the Upper Room which was hallowed by the memories of the Last Supper.

In this connexion we can see that the two

earlier appearances which have been recorded fulfilled an important preparatory function. Even though the tidings of those to whom they were granted did not produce a complete faith, yet they must have created expectancy and hope. 'The 'eleven and those that were with them' were ready in some degree to receive the Lord, as ready as men can be to face the powers of another world.

III.

[Mark]xvi. 13 f.

In the revelation of the Easter evening we have then a social revelation of the Lord; and it is presented to us by the Evangelists under the two aspects which have been already indicated. St Luke has chosen out of it those particular details which enable us to see how it wrought a public conviction of the reality of the Lord's Resurrection, of the absolute identity of Him that was crucified with Him that had overcome the grave; and so he establishes the true humanity of our heavenly King. St John again assumes all this as known, and goes on to recall the signs of sovereign majesty by which the first manifestation of Christ to His Church was accompanied; and so he establishes the Divine power of Christ's visible kingdom. There is, as will be seen afterwards, a minute contrast and correspondence between the two narratives. But I do not dwell on this now. I wish to speak only of the record of St Luke, and to consider by the xxiv. 36 ff.

III. help of his narrative how the Apostles were assured of that Gospel of the Resurrection which it was their work to preach, and how they were taught to interpret it.

One thing cannot fail to strike the reader when he compares the record of this manifestation with the narratives which have been already considered. Now for the first time we read of fear and disbelief being found in those who see the Lord. For a time Mary Magdalene and the two disciples failed to recognise Him. But when their eyes were opened their joy and their faith were perfect. The fulness of love, the intensity of purified understanding, cast out the instinctive terror which attaches to the sight of the unearthly. It was nothing to them that He whom they had found was instantly withdrawn. They knew in their own hearts that they had found Him. But, as we must observe, this assurance was for themselves. It was not of a kind which they could convey with certainty to others. The incredulous might say that they were enthusiasts and had seen a vision. And so in fact we read in general terms in the appendix to St Mark's Gospel, that they who heard Mary Magdalene's message 'disbelieved;' and that when the two told what had befallen them 'unto the rest, neither did they believe them.'

[Mark] xvi. 11.
id. 13.

Belief gained with difficulty. 65

It was then this general, this natural incredulity of men which was to be overcome; and those to whom the new revelation was given fairly represented the conditions under which such incredulity is found. Experience, hope, doubt, despondency, disbelief, were contending among them for the mastery. They were a mixed company in which there were manifold varieties of temperament and inclination. And so the Lord in His love met their requirements. The mode of His manifestation offered facilities for testing its character. Opportunity was given to all for realising and overcoming doubt. There was no room for mistake or for enthusiasm. The calm trust which was created in these first sceptics brings confidence to us.

III.

It has often been said, and it is said still, that the belief in the Lord's Resurrection was shaped and spread by those who were familiar with the idea and who were eager to find in it the fulfilment of their hopes. The narrative of St Luke, which is before us, is an answer by anticipation to such assertions. We see here in a vivid transcript from life that the idea of the Resurrection was strange and even alarming to the disciples as a body; we see that belief was enforced only after long resistance.

These facts are, as has been said, brought

III. before us in a transcript from life, in act and not in assertion; and the manner in which they are brought before us is singularly true to nature. It was evening and there was now quiet and leisure. The eleven and their companions were talking of the events of the day. They were evidently gathered together for counsel, or in some vague hope. *The Lord, they said one to another, hardly realising what they meant, is risen indeed. And as they spake these things [Jesus] Himself stood in the midst of them, and saith unto them, Peace be unto you.* Rebuke, discipline, instruction, came afterwards. The first words were words of loving encouragement. And the disciples had need of it. For their feelings were at once changed by what they saw. It is easy perhaps to speak of one coming to us from beyond the grave, but to be face to face with such a one is another thing. Flesh and blood must shrink from contact with the other world. This sudden, unprepared, mysterious appearance was not what even believers had looked for. *They were terrified and affrighted and supposed that they beheld a spirit.* How else could they explain His Presence in the midst when the doors were shut? He was simply there as they spoke of Him. And if *they knew not* in any sense *that He must rise from the dead*, it was as yet inconceivable that He should rise wholly

Luke xxiv. 36.

John xx. 9.

the power of a new life. 67

changed and yet wholly the same. They had distrusted others, and now they distrusted themselves. Nothing can be further removed from any precipitancy of belief; nothing can be less like hope taking shape as fact. Even so the Lord read their thoughts and answered them. He offered Himself to sight and touch. *Why, He asks, are ye troubled? and wherefore do reasonings arise in your hearts?* There is, He implies, a double trial for faith in the awfulness of all spiritual intercourse and in the difficulty of testing its certainty. But that world which I lay open is not such as you have shaped. *See my hands and my feet, that it is I myself. Handle me and see, for a spirit hath not flesh and bones, as ye behold me having. And while they still disbelieved for joy and wondered, He said unto them, Have ye anything to eat? And they gave Him a piece of a broiled fish; and He took it and did eat before them.*

We marked before what was the Apostles' doubt when the Lord came. The history of the Church is the witness to the faith which was produced by His coming. Slowly, jealously, almost reluctantly, the faith was embraced; and then it became henceforward the power of a new life.

We can at once see how it was so. The Risen

III. Christ was found to unite in His Person two worlds. The Apostles when He came to them thought that they beheld a spirit, not as once before on the Galilæan lake a mere phantom, but a Being of a different nature. His answer was, and is for all time: *Behold my hands and my feet that it is I myself:* I who lived for you, I who died for you, truly, perfectly, eternally man.

Such is the Truth which stands out as the foundation of the apostolic preaching. Christ who rose is the very same Christ who suffered. This assertion of identity is however guarded implicitly by the Evangelists against misunderstanding. Careful reflection will at once shew us that our bodies are nothing more than the outward expression of unseen forces, according to the laws of our present existence. If the medium, the element of existence be changed, the form in which the sum of these forces, which constitute the person, manifests itself will also be changed, changed because the person is the same. And so we see in the Gospels that the Risen Christ is, as I have said before, wholly changed while wholly the same: changed because He now belongs in His humanity to a new order. He can obey at His will the present laws of material being, but He is not bound by them.

truly man. 69

These considerations, though necessary if we wish to embrace the whole truth as it is revealed to us, are soon lost in mystery; and they lie in the background of the narrative of St Luke. But still they are indicated, not obscurely, if we compare the phrase *flesh and blood cannot inherit the kingdom of heaven* with the words which he has preserved: *a spirit hath not flesh and bones, as ye behold me having.* At the same time the main thought which St Luke connects with the first manifestation of the Risen Christ to His Church is that of His perfect humanity, and of His perfect humanity especially in connexion with His Passion. He teaches us to connect the issue of His agony with His work in triumph[1]. The prints of the nails are not only signs of recognition, but also signs of victory. Just as we have seen that the Lord in His discourse with the two disciples shewed the necessity of suffering as the condition of entrance to glory, so here He points to His wounded hands and feet, as proving that He bears even within the veil the tokens of redeeming love.

III.

1 Cor. xv. 50.

The conception is one on which Art has always loved to dwell. We must all have seen again and

---

[1] The same truth is indicated by the tense in St Matthew xxviii. 5, *Jesus which hath been crucified* ('Ιησοῦν τὸν ἐσταυρωμένον, not τὸν σταυρωθέντα). Comp. 1 Cor. i. 23; Gal. iii. 1.

70 *The vision of*

III. again figures of the Lord in Glory raising His wounded hands to bless, or pleading even on the throne of Judgment with those who have rejected Him by the marks of His Death, so shewing that by these He is still known: that by these He still proclaims the unchanging Gospel 'Redemption through sacrifice[1].'

But among the different shapes in which the thought has been embodied none, I think, is more striking than a vision which St Martin, the soldier-saint, related to have happened to himself. The terrible disorders of the times led faithful men to think then that the day of judgment must be at hand. Filled, as we may suppose, with such thoughts of the speedy coming of Christ's kingdom, the saint was one day, as he said, praying in his cell, when suddenly it was filled with a glorious light in the centre of which stood a figure of serene and joyous aspect clothed in royal array, with a jewelled crown upon his head, and gold embroidered shoes upon his feet. Martin at first was half-blinded by the sight; and for a time no word was spoken. Then his visitant said: 'Recognise, 'Martin, him whom thou beholdest. I am Christ.

[1] The thought finds a peculiar expression in the central boss of the western porch of Peterborough Cathedral, where the Father Himself raises, as it were, in the sight of the world the wounded hand of His Son.

St Martin. 71

'As I am about to descend to the earth, it is my III.
'pleasure to manifest myself to thee beforehand.'
When Martin made no reply, he continued, 'Why
'dost thou hesitate to believe, when thou seest?
'I am Christ.' Thereupon Martin, as by a sudden
inspiration, answered, 'The Lord Jesus did not
'foretell that He would come arrayed in purple
'and crowned with gold. I will not believe that
'Christ has come unless I see Him in the dress
'and shape in which He suffered, unless I see
'Him bear before my eyes the marks of the
'Cross.' Forthwith, so the story ends, the apparition vanished, and Martin knew that he had been tempted by the Evil One[1].

Now whatever else we may think of this remarkable legend, so much at least is certain, that the thought which it presents is most true. The conviction which was borne in upon the soul of that courageous confessor near fifteen centuries ago, when the world seemed to be hastening to its ruin, is no less precious now. A Christ without the Cross is no Saviour for us. The cross upon our foreheads is the token of our profession. The living emblems of the cross upon our Lord are the pledge of the fulfilment of His work. This is the first lesson of the appearance on the evening of Easter Day. He who rose and sits at the right

[1] Sulpicius Severus, *V. M.* xxv.

III. hand of God is 'the same Jesus' who suffered and died for us, the same in power of sympathy, the same in prevailing love.

If it were not so the very thought of the resurrection, the thought of the absolute permanence of character and actions, of all that is shaped in the heart or uttered by the lips, would be almost intolerable. That we shall live on with all the results of the past clinging to us, that we shall continue to be what we have slowly become day by day, is under all circumstances a prospect of overwhelming solemnity. But the revelation of the Risen Christ, bearing the tokens of His love unto death, enables us to look upon it without dismay. From that new order He has spoken the greeting of Peace. If our hearts fail us with natural fear, we can trust Him Who is greater than our hearts, trust Him Who leaving the throne of His glory stoops to strengthen the weakness of His suffering disciples, trust Him Who in the moment of His victory made Himself known as able to be touched with the feeling of our infirmities, trust Him Who, when the realities of the other world come upon us with startling and awful suddenness, still says unto us as unto the disciples of old: *Why are ye troubled, and wherefore do reasonings rise in your hearts? Behold my hands and my feet, that it is I myself.*

Acts vii. 56.

The virtue of His Passion remains indeed unaltered and unalterable. He proclaims still to us from the fulness of His Majesty for our guidance and for our strength: *I became dead, and behold I am alive for evermore. I became dead* that I might open to you the gates of heaven. *I am alive for evermore* that I may be with you all the days, through every conflict of earthly discipline.

IV.

THE GREAT COMMISSION.

Οὔσης οὖν ὀψίας τῇ ἡμέρᾳ ἐκείνῃ τῇ μιᾷ σαββάτων, καὶ τῶν θυρῶν κεκλεισμένων ὅπου ἦσαν οἱ μαθηταὶ διὰ τὸν φόβον τῶν Ἰουδαίων, ἦλθεν ὁ Ἰησοῦς καὶ ἔστη εἰς τὸ μέσον, καὶ λέγει αὐτοῖς Εἰρήνη ὑμῖν. καὶ τοῦτο εἰπὼν ἔδειξεν καὶ τὰς χεῖρας καὶ τὴν πλευρὰν αὐτοῖς. ἐχάρησαν οὖν οἱ μαθηταὶ ἰδόντες τὸν κύριον. εἶπεν οὖν αὐτοῖς [ὁ Ἰησοῦς] πάλιν Εἰρήνη ὑμῖν· καθὼς ἀπέσταλκέν με ὁ πατήρ, κἀγὼ πέμπω ὑμᾶς. καὶ τοῦτο εἰπὼν ἐνεφύσησεν καὶ λέγει αὐτοῖς Λάβετε πνεῦμα ἅγιον· ἄν τινων ἀφῆτε τὰς ἁμαρτίας ἀφέωνται αὐτοῖς· ἄν τινων κρατῆτε κεκράτηνται.

When therefore it was evening, on that day, the first day
*of the week, and when the doors were shut where the disciples
were, for fear of the Jews, Jesus came and stood in the midst,
and saith unto them, Peace be unto you. And when he had
said this, he shewed unto them both his hands and his side.
The disciples therefore were glad, when they saw the Lord.
Jesus therefore said to them again, Peace be unto you: as the
Father hath sent me, even so send I you. And when he had
said this, he breathed on them, and saith unto them, Receive
ye the Holy Ghost: whose soever sins ye forgive, they are
forgiven unto them; whose soever sins ye retain, they are
retained.*

JOHN xx. 19—23.

Τοῦ γνῶναι αὐτὸν καὶ τὴν δύναμιν τῆς ἀναστάσεως αὐτοῦ.

That I may know him, and the power of his resurrection.

PHIL. iii. 10.

WE have seen that St Luke and St John have preserved for us the two complementary aspects of the first appearance of the Risen Lord to the representatives of His Church. St Luke enables us to understand how He assured them of the reality of His Resurrection: how He offered His glorified humanity as the foundation of their abiding faith: how He gave them confidence in His unfailing sympathy, by shewing that He bore even to the throne of heaven the marks of His dying love. St John completes our view of this beginning of the Church. He sets before us clearly that the apprehension of the Gospel was at once followed by the charge to proclaim it: that the work of Christ finished in one sense was to be continued in another: that fresh powers were divinely provided for the fulfilment of fresh duties. St John, so to speak, begins where St Luke ends. In his narrative the joy of trembling expectation, which at first dared not believe, has passed into the joy of calm assurance, where there is no longer any question as to the Person of the Lord.

80 *The record of St John the complement*

IV. The disciples were convinced as to the present: they were enlightened as to the past: the future still lay before them uncertain and unexplained. *Jesus therefore said to them again, Peace be unto* Matt. x. *you.* The Lord Himself used the salutation which 12. He enjoined on His followers; and the greeting of Peace was repeated because it was now spoken to new men under new circumstances. In the short time which had passed since the Lord stood among Luke xxiv. *the eleven and those that were with them*, they had 33. been completely changed. The questionings, the doubts, the terrors by which they had been beset, were removed. They had tasted the powers of the spiritual world. They had gained peace for themselves, peace in the certainty that death had been overcome: peace in their restored fellowship with the Master whom they had lost: peace in the words of love which removed from them the burden of remorse and sin. But this was not all. There were fears and dangers without as well as within. The shut doors could not but remind them of a world hostile and powerful. And this world was to be met and conquered. Their communion with Christ was not yet made perfect. The message of Mary Magdalene forewarned them of a separation close at hand; yet they could not remain isolated or inactive. Therefore in the prospect of the vast work which they had not yet

of the record of St Luke.

attempted: using the strength of the personal faith which they had gained: starting from the vantage-ground of quickened hope and reaching forth at once to the last issues of Christian effort, *Jesus said to them again, Peace be unto you. As the Father hath sent me, even so send I you. And when He had said this, He breathed on them, and saith unto them, Receive ye the Holy Ghost: whosesoever sins ye forgive, they are forgiven unto them; whosesoever sins ye retain, they are retained.*

The words thus uttered are the charter of the Christian Church. They define its mission: they confirm its authority: they reveal its life. They have indeed been so much obscured by glosses, and distorted by controversy, and misused by usurping powers, that it is very difficult for us now to rise to the perception of their original grandeur and breadth. But without entering upon any doubtful discussions, it will be enough for us to direct our attention to two or three facts in connexion with the passage, in order to place it in a truer light than that in which it is commonly regarded.

1. The words were not addressed to all the apostles nor to the apostles alone. Thomas was absent; and there were others assembled with the apostles, as we learn from St Luke. The commission and the promise were given therefore, like the Pentecostal blessing which they prefigured, to

Luke xxiv. 23 f.

the Christian society and not to any special order in it.

2. The power which is described deals with sin and not with the punishment of sin. In essence it has nothing to do with discipline. It belongs to a spiritual world: and in regard to this it manifests the divine will and does not determine it.

3. The forgiveness and the retention of sins is represented as following from the impartment of a new being. The breathing upon the disciples recals, even in the word used to express it, that act of creative energy whereby God breathed into the first man the breath of life.

4. The gift is conveyed once for all. No provision is laid down for its transmission. It is made part of the life of the whole society, flowing from the relation of the body to the Risen Christ. Thus the words are, I repeat, the charter of the Christian Church, and not simply the charter of the Christian ministry. They complete what Christ had begun, and could only begin, before His Passion. He had given to His disciples the power of the keys to open the treasury of the kingdom of heaven and dispense things new and old. He had given them power to bind and to loose, to fix and to unfix ordinances for the government of the new society. And now as Conqueror

the charter of the Church. 83

He added the authority to deal with sins. In saying this I do not touch upon the divine necessity by which the different persons and channels through which the manifold graces of the Christian life are administered were afterwards marked out. I wish only to insist upon the apostolic mission of all Christians, which no subsequent delegation of specific duties to others can annul. And it is surely most remarkable that St John, by whom this commission is recorded, and St Peter, to whom representative power was given, stand out among the writers of the New Testament as dwelling on the priestly office of all Christians. All Christians, as such, are indeed apostles, envoys of their Risen Lord. To ministers and to people alike, while they are as yet undistinguished, He directs the words of sovereign power in the announcement of His victory over death and sin, *Peace be unto you: as the Father hath sent me, even so send I you. Receive ye the Holy Ghost: whosoever sins ye forgive, they are forgiven unto them; whosoever sins ye retain, they are retained.*

In this wider application of the words we can see a little more of the meaning of the last most mysterious clause. The message of the Gospel is the glad-tidings of sin conquered. To apply this to each man severally is the office of the Church, and so of each member of the Church. To embrace it personally is to gain absolution. As we in our different places bring home to the consciences of others the import of Christ's work, so far we set them free from the bondage in which they are held. There is therefore nothing arbitrary in the fulfilment of the divine promise. He to whom the word comes can appropriate or reject the message of deliverance which we as Christians are authorised to bear. As he does so, we, speaking in Christ's name, either remove the load by which he is weighed down or make it more oppressive. For the preaching of Christ cannot leave men as it finds them. If it does not bring true peace, it disturbs the false peace into which they have fallen. To this end all the sacraments and ordinances of Christianity combine, to deepen the conviction of sin and to announce the forgiveness of sin. In one way or other they bring before the world the living lessons of the Passion and of the Resurrection. And we all are charged to interpret them.

As the Father hath sent me, even so send I you. The exact form of the language is most significant. Generally the words express a resemblance of character between the mission of Christ and the mission of His apostles, and, not merely a resemblance of form. At the same time there is a difference between the two verbs

to the mission of Christ. 85

equally translated 'send' which cannot be overlooked. The first marks a definite work to be done; the second a personal relation of the sender and the sent. And in this connexion it is important to notice that Christ speaks of His mission as present and not as past, as continuing and not as concluded. He says, *As the Father hath sent me*, and not merely *as the Father sent me*. He declares, that is, that His work is not over, though the manner in which it is done is changed. Henceforth He is and He acts in those whom He has chosen. They are in Him sharing in the fulness of His power: He is in them sharing in the burden of their labours. The promise of the Last Supper, the prayer on the way to Gethsemane, are accomplished. The disciples have entered on their inheritance of peace. They have beheld the glory of the Lord. And now it is their part to bear witness, that the world may believe.

We have only to realise the change which was wrought in the disciples within the short hours of the first Easter Day, in order that we may understand the substance and the authority of this witness which they had to give. They had known the defeat of death; they had received forgiveness; they had felt the breath of a divine life. Christ had inspired them with the power of His glorified manhood. He had given them the Holy

Spirit through Himself. It was then their office to proclaim their experience, each according to the measure of his gift. And that office remains to be fulfilled as long as the Christian society exists. From the time of the apostles ever onwards the same blessings have been imparted to every generation of believers, and the blessings have brought and still bring with them the same obligations.

The fact lies at the foundation of our spiritual being. It is true that in the providential ordering of the Christian society various functions and graces have been variously concentrated; but all belong alike to the new life which the Risen Christ breathed into His Church. And whoever has consciously felt this life stirring within him, whoever has felt that it has brought rest in the midst of conflicts and light in the hour of gloom, whoever has felt that the faith in Christ's glorified humanity gives unity to the broken fragments of labour, and clothes our fleeting days with an eternal beauty, has heard, heard as truly as the disciples in the upper chamber, the words of the Lord: *As the Father hath sent me, even so send I you.*

As the Father hath sent me. Christ comes *not to destroy but to fulfil,* not to sweep away all the growths of the past, but to carry to its proper consummation every undeveloped germ of right. Even so He sends us to take our stand in the midst of things as they are: to guard with tender thoughtfulness all that has been consecrated to His service, and to open the way for the many powers which work together for His glory. Christ came in His Father's name, not of Himself, nor to do His own will. *Though He was Son, yet learned He obedience by the things which He suffered.* Waiting till the hour came, He bore all that the hour brought. Even so He sends us to crush down the promptings of our self-will, to discipline our impatience, to wait as well as to work, to listen for that divine voice which is articulate only to the still watchings of faith.

Heb. v. 8.

Christ came *not to be ministered unto but to minister, and to give His life a ransom for many;* not to win an easy battle, but to redeem through apparent defeat. Even so He sends us to reap what we have not sown, to sow what we shall not reap, to strive to learn and to work as believing that sacrifice alone is fruitful.

Christ came not to judge but to save, and still He came for a judgment; not *to send peace upon the earth, but fire and a sword.* His will was perfect love, but He did not veil the terrible law of His word, which kills if it does not quicken.

88 The work of the Church

iv. Even so He sends us. The message which we have to bear will make the chains of evil more galling if it does not break them. The message of the Resurrection may be a message of peace: it may be a message of condemnation.

Christ came as *a light into the world*, bringing from another realm that which earth could not furnish, to illuminate, to vivify, to guide. Even so He sends us. We dare not dissemble that we are entrusted with a supernatural message. We have that to make known which is not of the world, but above it: that which cannot be measured or tested by limited standards: that which justifies itself simply by shining.

Christ came *to bear witness to the Truth:* to claim as His own everything that *is:* to claim the allegiance of every one that is of the Truth. Even so He sends us. In His name we take possession of every fact which is established by thought or inquiry. We fail in duty, we fail in faith, if we allow any human interest, or endowment, or acquisition to lie without the domain of the Cross.

Christ came *to seek and to save that which was lost, to call not righteous but sinners to repentance.* Even so He sends us to dare something for the Gospel, to believe that it has a power to arrest the careless, to raise the fallen, to find an answer in dull cold hearts, to move by a divine sympathy those whom the counsels of reason cannot reach.

As the Father hath sent me. Christ came to perfect, to serve, to enlighten. Such is the universal Christian mission. As we understand its character the knowledge becomes in us a spring of supplication; for the world around us shews that there is grievous need that we should all hear the divine call and answer it. The special duties, privileges, responsibilities of the Christian ministry remain undiminished and undisparaged when we recognise the common priesthood of all believers as sharers in the Life of the Risen Lord and charged to make known that which they have experienced. The greatest danger of the Church at present seems to be not lest we should forget the peculiar functions of ministerial office, but lest we should allow this to supersede the general power which it concentrates and represents in the economy of life. If only every Christian would have the courage to confess what he has found in his faith, simply and soberly, without affection and without reserve; if that is, our apostles were multiplied a thousandfold; we should not wait so sadly, so doubtingly, as we do, for the last triumph of Christ: we should rejoice to *hasten His Coming*, when He shall return in

2 Pet. iii. 12.

IV. glory, the same Jesus who died and rose from the dead: we should, in a sense which we have not yet felt, *know Him and the power of His Resurrection.*

V.

SPIRITUAL SIGHT.

Θωμᾶc δὲ εἷc ἐκ τῶν δώδεκα, ὁ λεγόμενος Δίδυ-
μος, οὐκ ἦν μετ' αὐτῶν ὅτε ἦλθεν Ἰηcοῦc. ἔλεγον
οὖν αὐτῷ οἱ ἄλλοι μαθηταί Ἑωράκαμεν τὸν κύριον.
ὁ δὲ εἶπεν αὐτοῖc Ἐὰν μὴ ἴδω ἐν ταῖc χερcὶν αὐτοῦ
τὸν τύπον τῶν ἥλων καὶ βάλω τὸν δάκτυλόν μου εἰc
τὸν τύπον τῶν ἥλων καὶ βάλω μου τὴν χεῖρα εἰc
τὴν πλευρὰν αὐτοῦ, οὐ μὴ πιcτεύcω. Καὶ μεθ' ἡμέρας
ὀκτὼ πάλιν ἦcαν ἔcω οἱ μαθηταὶ αὐτοῦ καὶ Θωμᾶc
μετ' αὐτῶν. ἔρχεται ὁ Ἰηcοῦc τῶν θυρῶν κεκλειcμέ-
νων, καὶ ἔcτη εἰc τὸ μέcον καὶ εἶπεν Εἰρήνη ὑμῖν.
εἶτα λέγει τῷ Θωμᾷ Φέρε τὸν δάκτυλόν cου ὧδε
καὶ ἴδε τὰc χεῖράc μου, καὶ φέρε τὴν χεῖρά cου καὶ
βάλε εἰc τὴν πλευράν μου, καὶ μὴ γίνου ἄπιcτοc ἀλλὰ
πιcτόc. ἀπεκρίθη Θωμᾶc καὶ εἶπεν αὐτῷ Ὁ κύριόc
μου καὶ ὁ θεόc μου. λέγει αὐτῷ [ὁ] Ἰηcοῦc Ὅτι
ἑώρακάc με πεπίcτευκαc; μακάριοι οἱ μὴ ἰδόντες καὶ
πιcτεύcαντες.

But Thomas, one of the twelve, called Didymus, was not with them when Jesus came. The other disciples therefore said unto him, We have seen the Lord. But he said unto them, Except I shall see in his hands the print of the nails, and put my finger into the print of the nails, and put my hand into his side, I will not believe.

And after eight days again his disciples were within, and Thomas with them. Jesus cometh, the doors being shut, and stood in the midst, and said, Peace be unto you. Then saith he to Thomas, Reach hither thy finger, and see my hands; and reach hither thy hand, and put it into my side: and be not faithless, but believing. Thomas answered and said unto him, My Lord and my God. Jesus saith unto him, Because thou hast seen me, thou hast believed: blessed are they that have not seen, and yet have believed.

JOHN xx. 24—29.

Μακάριοι οἱ καθαροὶ τῇ καρδίᾳ, ὅτι αὐτοὶ τὸν Θεὸν ὄψονται.

Blessed are the pure in heart, for they shall see God.
MATT. v. 8.

SPIRITUAL SIGHT.

THE first Easter Day witnessed, as we have seen, the fulfilment of the victory of the Risen Lord. Within the brief space of a few hours He satisfied the great needs of individual believers and of the Church at large. He brought in His own Person joy to the bereaved, understanding to the ignorant, forgiveness to the denier. He gave to the Church the clear apprehension of the Gospel of the Resurrection, and full authority to proclaim it. But in this triumph of the new life there was one dark spot. *Thomas, we read, one of the twelve, was not with them* [the disciples] *when Jesus came.* By that absence he missed the blessing which the others gained. It is impossible to determine certainly why he kept away from the little assembly of waiting disciples; but we can be sure that the cause lay in himself. We read in an earlier chapter of the Gospel that he had come up to Jerusalem, as he believed, to die with Christ; and Christ was now dead. He had thought again on the eve of the Passion that if he had known Christ's end he should have

v.

John xi. 16.

John xiv. 5.

known the way of which He spoke. The way was now only too sadly clear, and the end (he might argue) must be like it. Thomas in the face of that terrible scene upon the Cross, the details of which were vividly present to his mind, found nothing more to hope. It may well have seemed best to him to be alone and to prepare silently for the worst. So while he brooded over his own thoughts, Christ fulfilled His promise elsewhere to the two or three gathered together in His name. But the sorrow of the one was not forgotten in the general gladness. The ten did not keep their good news for themselves. *The other disciples therefore said* (ἔλεγον) *unto him, We have seen the Lord.* Again and again, so the words imply, they repeated their message, unfolding, as we must believe, all that was involved in the simple expression of the fact, their fears, their misgivings, their conviction, their commission, insisting on the several details which were best fitted to move him to faith. But to their pleadings he has only one answer: *He said* (εἶπεν) *unto them, Except I shall see in His hands the print of the nails, and put my finger into the print of the nails, and put my hand into His side, I will not believe.* If they had seen and touched, he must see and touch too. Nothing less could suffice. The wounds, by which they had recognised the

Lord, were for him the gaping wounds of the death which he had witnessed. Unless these, such as he had looked upon them, could be reconciled with life, faith for him was impossible. And the form in which his thought is expressed seems to exclude hope. *Except I shall see*, he says, *I will not;* and not rather with yearning expectation, *If I see, I will*[1].

In this way the disciples as a body were met by the same incredulity which they had themselves shewn to the earliest heralds of the Resurrection. They could hardly fail to remember how the words of the women had seemed to them to be idle tales. So true it is that the first preaching of the Gospel called out the main objection which is urged still. The question was asked from the first: How can such things be believed on the word of others? The difficulty is not one which has been brought to light recently. It is as old as Christianity. And the test which Thomas proposed is like those which are often lightly talked of now. We shall soon see how the difficulty was met, the test overpassed.

---

[1] It must be added that the satisfaction of the test would have involved a complete change in the Body of the Lord. So St Thomas asked for something which went beyond his own thoughts.

v. But before touching on the sequel of the history we must notice the solemn pause which succeeded to the joyful excitement of Easter Day. A time of discipline followed the time of revelation. For a whole week, as far as we know, after those first few hours, the Lord was not seen. Those who had believed were left to ponder over and interpret and fit into life the facts which they had gained. He who could not believe was left to examine calmly and patiently the grounds of his doubt. To us perhaps the silence and the suspense seem strange; but in such great matters there is large room for patience. We do grievous wrong to spiritual sensibility when we seek to hasten the momentous crises of faith. During the space of quiet reflection and calm communing, belief, as we cannot question, grew more gentle without losing its power, and doubt grew less defiant without disguising its difficulties. So the seven days of the Paschal feast came to an end. The sabbath followed, on which it was impossible to leave Jerusalem. Then came the second Lord's Day on which the disciples were at length free to go to Galilee according to Christ's command. But yet they did not go at once. They lingered still in the Holy City.. It may have been that they had a vague sense that this was to be their weekly festival; it may have

Christ's return.

been that they awaited with a dim hope that now once more the Risen Lord would appear to them before they left the scene of their great sorrow and their great joy. At any rate *after eight days again His disciples were within,* doubtless in the same upper room, *and Thomas with them.* He had therefore not withdrawn from their company even though he could not share their gladness; they had not refused to admit him among them, though his unbelief threw a shadow over their assurance. So while they may have been again talking of the marvels of Easter Day, *Jesus cometh, the doors being shut, and stood in the midst, and said, Peace be unto you.* We can easily imagine that these words were sufficient; that in that loving Presence Thomas forgot the test which he had laid down: that he shrank back behind his fellow-apostles, as thoughts flashed upon him which he had been unable to entertain before. But it was needful that all should be laid bare before he could be fully healed. The Lord had given His common blessing of peace. *Then saith He to Thomas, Reach hither thy finger, and see my hands: and reach hither thy hand, and put it into my side: and be not faithless, but believing.* He had heard then the very phrases in which Thomas had fashioned the defence of his doubt. At the time

v. when the Apostle was questioning the Resurrection of his Lord, the Lord was listening to him unseen. And now when with infinite condescension the Lord offers what had been demanded, the Apostle feels how immeasurably his test had fallen below what he had reached. The immediate consciousness of the unchanged love of his Master, of His penetrating knowledge, of His living sympathy, of His sovereign majesty, raised him at once into a new region. With one bound he is borne upwards to the vision of the highest truth. Refusing, as is evident from the whole tenour of the history, to accept the satisfaction of His own condition, *Thomas answered and said unto Him: My Lord and my God.* Thus he was strengthened to make a confession which no one had made before. No testimony of sense, of sight and touch, could have established such a conviction. Flesh and blood had not revealed it to him, but his Father in heaven. He who had doubted, he who had honestly if rashly given utterance to his doubts, now with equal courage dares to say what he feels, that his Lord is his God also. And Christ receives the homage. Thomas had longed to gain conviction of the manhood of the Risen Lord, and he is privileged to declare His Divinity. He enjoyed, as far as it can be enjoyed on earth, the

the blessing of the later Church. 101

blessing of the pure in heart, and saw God. As we now look upon the whole narrative we can see that the Apostle had indeed answered to his Master's discipline. He had in a sense other than he had foreseen not only 'died with Him,' but also risen again. Through sharp and lonely experience he had found out what external evidence can do, and what it cannot do. He had made his own terms and he had known their insufficiency. By his bitter sorrow he has shewed us a more excellent way. He doubted, as has been well said, that we may not doubt: he doubted for the more confirmation of our faith.

It remains then for us to enjoy the fruit of his experience. *Jesus saith unto him, Because thou hast seen me thou hast believed*—or perhaps better with a half sad question: *Because thou hast seen me hast thou believed? blessed are they that have not seen and yet have believed.* Some there were even in that company, so the original implies, who could take to themselves the blessing; some who had heard the Easter tidings and welcomed them with childlike joy. And from the hour when the blessing was first pronounced there have been in every age a multitude, whom no man can number, who have known its unspeakable power. One illustration from life is sufficient to reveal the thoughts of many hearts. When Dr Arnold was suddenly stricken with his mortal agony, he was seen, we are told, lying still, with "his hands clasped, his lips "moving, and his eyes raised upwards, as if "engaged in prayer, when all at once he repeated, "firmly and earnestly, 'And Jesus said unto him, "'Thomas, because thou hast seen thou hast be-"'lieved: blessed are they who have not seen and "'yet have believed.'"

Here then lies the central lesson of this revelation of the Risen Lord, the revelation of His spiritual presence, the revelation of man's spiritual sight. The truest, serenest, happiest faith is within our reach. We have not lost more than we have gained by the removal of the events of the Gospel history far from our own times. The last beatitude of the Gospel is the special endowment of the later Church. The testimony of sense given to the Apostles, like the testimony of word given to us, is but the starting-point of faith. The substance of faith is not a fact which we cannot explain away, or a conclusion which we cannot escape, but the personal apprehension of a living, loving Friend. And Christ still makes Himself known in His Church and in each believer's heart by words of peace. He is still with us the same as eighteen hundred years ago, unchanged and unchangeable, the same yesterday, to-day, and for ever. But while this is so: while no outward effort, no force of argument, can carry us into the region which contains the object of faith, we must notice how tenderly the Lord deals with the doubter who is ready to believe, and with what wise tolerance the Christian society keeps within its pale him whom a ruthless logic might have declared to be a denier of the Gospel. The society continues the gift of a soothing fellowship. The Lord places within the reach of him who had not ceased to be a disciple the evidence which He asks. By such help he was enabled to rise above himself. If indeed the Risen Christ had been no more than Thomas could have proved by his touch, then indeed the very fulfilment of his test would have destroyed the Apostle's real hope. As it was, he gained the conviction which he sought, and through this the Lord called him to a better mind.

Be not faithless, Christ said, *but believing.* Doubts are not unbelief, and yet they open the way to unbelief. If they are not resolutely faced, if they are allowed to float about like unsubstantial shadows, if they are alleged as excuses for the neglect of practical duties, if they are cherished as

v. Hebr. xiii. 8.

v. signs of superior intelligence, the history of St Thomas has no encouragement for those who feel them. The Lord revealed Himself to Thomas not while he kept himself apart in proud isolation, or in lonely despondency, but when he was joined to the company of his fellow-apostles, though he could not share their confidence. Doubts are often dallied with: and still worse, they are often affected. It is strange that the hypocrisy of scepticism should be looked upon as less repulsive than the affectation of belief, yet in the present day it has become almost a fashion for men to repeat doubts on the gravest questions without the least sense of personal responsibility. Nothing is more common than to be told by easy talkers that this is impossible and that that has been disproved, when a very little inquiry will shew that these doubters upon trust have never even seriously attempted to examine the conditions of the problems which they presume to decide. For such hope lies in a spiritual conversion. Christ has no promises for dishonest doubt any more than for unreal faith.

But there are real doubts; and if any are perplexed by difficulties which they feel to be an actual burden and sorrow, for them the revelation to St Thomas has a message of hope. Let these have patience under their trial; let them gain,

Doubts faced. 105

if they can, some spaces for quiet thought; let them consider carefully how far their difficulties belong necessarily to the subject to which they attach; let them try to conceive some way by which the difficulties could have been avoided; and then when they have arranged all, let them count up the loss and gain on this imaginary plan. The result will be, if the past can be trusted, that they will find signs of a Divine presence and a Divine foresight even in that which has perplexed them.

Christianity shrinks from no test while it transcends all. If therefore doubts come we must not dally with them or put them by, but bring them into a definite form, and question them. And in God's good time they will, as of old, prove an occasion for fuller, unanticipated knowledge. The words stand written for the latest age: *Be not*, or more literally, *Become not faithless, but believing*. *Become not*: the final issues of faith and unbelief are slowly reached. But there is no stationariness in the spiritual life. We must at each moment either be moving forwards to fuller assurance and clearer vision, or backwards to a dull insensibility. We may discern little; we may think that the prospect is closed against us by insuperable barriers; but if our eyes are steadily turned towards the light, if we love the

v. Lord's appearing, He will reveal Himself at last. We shall then see that which we have by sin lost the power of seeing now. The eye of the spirit will see what the eye of flesh cannot see. As yet the Fall has left us blind, though we can still hear the voice of God in the stillness of the soul[1]. We hear His voice though we cannot see His shape. But it will not always be so. The blessing of faith shall be crowned by the blessing of fruition. The Risen Christ will fulfil His own benediction: *Blessed are the pure in heart, for they shall see God.*

[1] This thought finds a most striking expression in two lines of a Coventry Miracle Play (quoted by Dr Macdonald, *England's Antiphon*, p. 25). Adam replies to the Divine question after the Fall,

'Ah Lord! for sin our flowers do fade:
I hear Thy voice, but I see Thee nought.'

VI.

THE REVELATION IN THE WORK OF LIFE.

πρωίας δε Ηδη γινομένης έστη Ἰησοῦς εἰς τὸν
αἰγιαλόν· οὐ μέντοι ᾔδεισαν οἱ μαθηταὶ ὅτι Ἰησοῦς
ἐστίν. λέγει οὖν αὐτοῖς Ἰησοῦς Παιδία, μή τι προσ-
φάγιον ἔχετε; ἀπεκρίθησαν αὐτῷ Οὔ· ὁ δὲ εἶπεν
αὐτοῖς Βάλετε εἰς τὰ δεξιὰ μέρη τοῦ πλοίου τὸ
δίκτυον, καὶ εὑρήσετε. ἔβαλον οὖν, καὶ οὐκέτι αὐτὸ
ἑλκύσαι ἴσχυον ἀπὸ τοῦ πλήθους τῶν ἰχθύων. λέγει
οὖν ὁ μαθητὴς ἐκεῖνος ὃν ἠγάπα ὁ Ἰησοῦς τῷ
Πέτρῳ Ὁ κύριός ἐστιν. Σίμων οὖν Πέτρος, ἀκού-
σας ὅτι ὁ κύριός ἐστιν, τὸν ἐπενδύτην διεζώσατο,
ἦν γὰρ γυμνός, καὶ ἔβαλεν ἑαυτὸν εἰς τὴν θάλασσαν·
οἱ δὲ ἄλλοι μαθηταὶ τῷ πλοιαρίῳ ἦλθον, οὐ γὰρ
ἦσαν μακρὰν ἀπὸ τῆς γῆς ἀλλὰ ὡς ἀπὸ πηχῶν
διακοσίων, σύροντες τὸ δίκτυον τῶν ἰχθύων. Ὡς οὖν
ἀπέβησαν εἰς τὴν γῆν βλέπουσιν ἀνθρακιὰν κειμένην
καὶ ὀψάριον ἐπικείμενον καὶ ἄρτον. λέγει αὐτοῖς [ὁ]
Ἰησοῦς Ἐνέγκατε ἀπὸ τῶν ὀψαρίων ὧν ἐπιάσατε νῦν.
ἀνέβη οὖν Σίμων Πέτρος καὶ εἵλκυσεν τὸ δίκτυον εἰς
τὴν γῆν μεστὸν ἰχθύων μεγάλων ἑκατὸν πεντήκοντα
τριῶν· καὶ τοσούτων ὄντων οὐκ ἐσχίσθη τὸ δίκτυον.
λέγει αὐτοῖς [ὁ] Ἰησοῦς Δεῦτε ἀριστήσατε. οὐδεὶς
ἐτόλμα τῶν μαθητῶν ἐξετάσαι αὐτὸν Σὺ τίς εἶ;
εἰδότες ὅτι ὁ κύριός ἐστιν. ἔρχεται Ἰησοῦς καὶ λαμ-
βάνει τὸν ἄρτον καὶ δίδωσιν αὐτοῖς, καὶ τὸ ὀψάριον
ὁμοίως. Τοῦτο ἤδη τρίτον ἐφανερώθη Ἰησοῦς τοῖς
μαθηταῖς ἐγερθεὶς ἐκ νεκρῶν.

But when day was now breaking, Jesus stood on the beach: howbeit the disciples knew not that it was Jesus. Jesus therefore saith unto them, Children, have ye aught to eat? They answered him, No. And he said unto them, Cast the net on the right side of the boat, and ye shall find. They cast therefore, and now they were not able to draw it for the multitude of fishes. That disciple therefore whom Jesus loved saith unto Peter, It is the Lord. So when Simon Peter heard that it was the Lord, he girt his coat about him (for he was naked), and cast himself into the sea. But the other disciples came in the little boat (for they were not far from the land, but about two hundred cubits off), dragging the net full of fishes. So when they got out upon the land, they see a fire of coals there, and fish laid thereon, and bread. Jesus saith unto them, Bring of the fish which ye have now taken. Simon Peter therefore went up, and drew the net to land, full of great fishes, a hundred and fifty and three: and for all there were so many, the net was not rent. Jesus saith unto them, Come and break your fast. And none of the disciples durst inquire of him, Who art thou? knowing that it was the Lord. Jesus cometh, and taketh the bread, and giveth them, and the fish likewise. This is now the third time that Jesus was manifested to the disciples, after that he was risen from the dead.

JOHN xxi. 1—14.

Οὐκ ἀφήσω ὑμᾶς ὀρφανούς, ἔρχομαι πρὸς ὑμᾶς.
I will not leave you desolate: I come unto you.
JOHN xiv. 18.

THE REVELATION IN THE WORK OF LIFE.

WE are now brought to the beginning of a new series of Revelations of the Risen Christ, which the Revelation made to St Thomas serves to introduce. Hitherto Christ has for the most part so made Himself known as to convince His disciples that hereafter their fellowship with Him would be perfected in some new fashion: that it behoved Him to suffer: that He was wholly the same if wholly changed: that they were empowered to carry forward in His stead and by His commission the work which He had begun. The Revelation to St Thomas was so far like the Revelations of Easter-Day that it was given to call out personal faith by sensible signs; yet it did this in such a way as to make clear the fact that Christ is most truly with His Church by an invisible spiritual presence, by an abiding spiritual power. It claimed the exercise of a spiritual sense in man for the apprehension of the Lord's true nature.

VI.

It brought the promise of a special blessing on the age to come. In the Revelations which followed, so far as they have been recorded in detail, the Lord throws light upon that mysterious future. He comes to those who are familiar with the truth of His Resurrection. He comes no longer to create faith, but to point out some salient features in the history of the propagation of the faith, *speaking*, as it is summed up in the Acts, *the things concerning the Kingdom of God*. The central thoughts are no more connected with the Passion and the Old Testament, but with the Return and the progress of the Church.

Acts i. 3.

Thus the whole scope of the revelation of the Risen Christ is changed, and for a time the scene is changed also. The two appearances recorded after that on the second Lord's Day took place in Galilee. The lake and the mountain which had witnessed the beginning of Christ's preparatory teaching were again chosen to witness the beginning of His work in glory. And even in these outward details there is a correspondence and a harmony which ought not to be overlooked. They help to place us at the right point of sight for interpreting the lessons which lie beneath.

This is obviously true with regard to the narrative of the second miraculous draught of fishes in the last chapter of St John's Gospel.

The narrative is so like and yet so unlike the corresponding narrative in St Luke, that we feel that they must preserve two aspects of the same spiritual truth: that the one is designed to help us to understand the other: that those who connected their call to be fishers of men with the first, must have found in the second a fuller and more joyful parable of their office. It lies upon the surface that the one history presents the office of the apostles in relation to the Christ still battling on earth: the other in relation to the same Christ victorious over death. Then the Lord was with them on the waters: here He stands upon the beach while they do His bidding. There the net began to break and the ships to sink: here though the fish *were so many the net was not rent*. There St Peter, when he dimly felt who He was that had wrought the work, prayed Him to depart from him, as unable to endure His holy Presence: here *when he heard that it was the Lord*, he cast himself into the sea, as unwilling to wait even until the vessel could carry him to the Saviour whom he had regained.

But without dwelling further upon these differences, which each one can trace out for himself, I would rather observe generally how in this history the old places, and the old work, and the

VI. old necessities are again used and ennobled in the light of the Resurrection. The sea of Galilee, by which the multitudes had gathered to hear the word, and whose waves Christ had stilled on the stormy night, once more is hallowed by His Presence. The fisherman's labour once more is taken as a lively image of apostolic toil in *the* Apoc. xvii. *many waters, which are peoples and multitudes* 1, 15. *and nations.* The fruitless efforts confessed once more call out the word of power and blessing. The Risen Christ shews Himself once more to be the same, guiding, disciplining, cheering His followers as aforetime, even if in another form.

And this appears to be the characteristic lesson of this particular manifestation. It is the sign which lays open to us Christ's action through the common course of life. He is recognised not by His Person but by His working. The gift of success and the gift of refreshment are seen to belong to Him and to make Him known.

This will appear clearly if we follow the narrative. There had been, so far as we know, another period of loneliness and silence in the experience of the Church, but this time without the sorrow of one doubt. The disciples had returned to Galilee, waiting for the fulfilment of the promise of the Easter Morning. Meanwhile they resumed their abandoned craft; and there is something sublime in the trustful patience with which they thus calmly went back to ordinary business in the prospect of the great future ready to be revealed. Never would it have been more natural for men to thrust all common occupations into the background: to yield to the absorbing thoughts of the Divine Presence which they had realised and of the unknown destiny to which they were called: to forget the simple claims of daily life. But past discipline had at least taught those who knew Christ best to wait. And during this time of solemn suspense there was nothing out of harmony with the true conception of their position, when St Peter said to the little group assembled together with him, *I go a fishing*, and they answered at once, *We also go with thee*. It seems indeed that this had been their custom since their return to their old home, for it is said *on that night they caught nothing*, as though there was something unusual in their ill success. Perhaps their failure may have recalled the like occurrence three short years before, which had been the turning-point of their lives. So much they knew that their own efforts were in vain. *But when day was now breaking*—the time described is the first beginning of dawn—*Jesus stood on the beach: howbeit the disciples knew not that it was Jesus.* Even though their hearts must have been full of

Him, there was nothing in the Stranger a hundred yards off by the waterside to suggest that this was He. Nor did His voice reveal Him to them as at first to Mary Magdalene. He would now *manifest Himself* in some other way, not by the personal address, not by the prints of nail and spear, but by His works to the seeing heart. So the command was given and obeyed. The blessing followed; and at once *the disciple whom Jesus loved*—he who was in closest sympathy with Him —saith unto Peter, *It is the Lord*, not 'my Lord' or 'our Lord,' still less 'our Master,' but with the fullest recognition of His authority, *It is the Lord*. Tried by the ordinary processes of reasoning, the conclusion was precarious. But there is a logic of the soul which deals with questions of the higher life, and St John trusted it. He recognised the insight, the power, the love which belonged to One only. And when the truth found utterance the others acknowledged it.

The sign was given: the lesson was read: the net *full of great fishes* was drawn unbroken to the land. Part of the prize had been rendered to the Lord. Then followed a new marvel. *Jesus saith unto them, Come and breakfast:* 'breakfast' and not 'dine,' as in preparation for the day's work and not in refreshment after it. The disciples had seen a fire when they landed and fish laid

the interpretation of acts. 117

thereon and bread. He who had asked them for meat and had taken of what they had caught had not needed their assistance. But Christ demands much when He is about to do much. And while they had worked, He had provided for them. He required their labour and not the fruits of their labour. He was Himself their host, waiting to give rather than to receive. By this fresh act they saw again who the Stranger must be. They would without doubt gladly have heard from His own lips the familiar words, 'It is I.' But it was His will at present to speak only by what He did. And *none of the disciples durst inquire of Him, Who art Thou? knowing that it was the Lord*. Then once again as He had fed the multitudes by their hand, on the borders of the same lake, He now feeds them: *He cometh and taketh the bread and giveth them, and the fish likewise.*

It would be easy to point out spiritual types in the circumstances of this morning meal of the Lord, which stands in striking contrast to the Last Supper, but such topics are best reserved for private study. It is more important now that we should notice the conditions under which the Lord *was manifested* this *third time* to the representatives of His Church. All the revelations of the Risen Christ are, as we have seen, helps towards the realisation of His true but invisible Presence with ourselves; and this one teaches us to know Him both in the history of the Church and in the brief course of our own lives by the blessings which follow obedience to His word. It appears that even to the last the disciples 'knew 'the Lord' only through the interpretation which they put upon their own experience. Not till afterwards did Christ speak so as to shew Himself to them in word. The meal, as it seems, was eaten in silence. No thanksgiving was pronounced. The revelation, as has been already said, was clear to the seeing heart. Without patient obedience, without cheerful labour, without loving insight, those to whom the Lord came would not have known Him. He would have been to them only as one mere chance wayfarer who had crossed their path. This is the uniform law. *The world beholdeth Me no more, but ye behold Me*, is the final promise to the faithful. At His first miracle Christ manifested His glory, and *His disciples*—His disciples and not others—*believed on Him*. Here at His last miracle He *manifested Himself*, He *was manifested*, according to His pleasure, and faith apprehended Him. It was in vain that His brethren, in a moment of unbelief, bade Him *manifest Himself to the world*. From the world which has not the will to obey, or

The condition of waiting. 119

the eye to see, the true Christ, the Risen Christ, must be always hidden.

The lesson is one which we cannot afford to neglect. Day by day the circumstances of that night and that morning on the Galilæan lake are being repeated among ourselves. Signs of Christ's Presence are offered to us which we can read or leave unregarded. And if we would look upon Him, as He stands on the solid shore while we are still tossed upon the waters, we must wait and work and obey. Then, though the night be long, He will manifest Himself to us as the day breaks.

We must wait. If we reflect, this is perhaps the lesson of the Great Forty Days, which will strike us most. The weeks of silence which intervened in that brief period of watching are marvellously eloquent. And as it was then it is still. We cannot prescribe the time for the Divine Appearance. Perhaps we need to learn and to feel that we are alone. There are seasons in the history of the Church and in our own lives when *there is no open vision*. There are seasons again of refreshment and preparation, when the voice of the Lord comes to us above the storm, it may be, or through the still calm. But Christ is no nearer at one time than at the other, and our

1 Sam. iii. 1.

The conditions of working

VI.
1 Sam. iii. 9.

one prayer should rise unceasingly: *Speak, Lord, for Thy servant heareth,* as Thou wilt, when Thou wilt.

We must work. We must pursue our appointed task, till a new command comes. It may seem a poor and dull thing to go back from scenes of great excitement and lofty expectation to simple duties which belonged to an earlier time. But that, we see, is the method of God. Perhaps it will be through these that the higher call will come: perhaps no higher call will ever come to us. But our duty is still the same. We cannot tell the value of any particular service either for the society or for our own training. Much must be done to the end of the workman's life, which is a preparation only. The Baptist continued to labour as he had first laboured,

John iii. 30.

though he knew and confessed, *I must decrease.*

We must obey. The order is given at last (so we are inclined to fancy), at an ill-chosen moment. We are wearied with long and fruitless toil. The favourable time has passed. We think that experience has made us acquainted with the conditions of hope, and we hope no longer. Moreover the order is given by one whom we do not recognise. But nevertheless it is clear and precise. We remember past crises not unlike that in which we are placed, when such an order was

and of obedience.

proved to be divine. And happy are we if we dare to trust the bidding which sounds in our hearts, to acknowledge the special call which brings home to us that vague, general, Presence in which we profess to believe. Then in the sequel of late and unlooked for success, as it may be, we shall know Him from whom it came.

In one sense it will be always true that we shall toil in the night: true that the gathering of the Church will be in the night: true that we shall be tempted to say within ourselves, *We have taken nothing.* Even so we can strive, God helping us, to *win our own souls in patience,* and to win souls for Him, till the day break and the shadows depart, waiting, working, obeying; and on the Great Morning, when there *shall be no more sea,* no more storm and peril and change, the Lord will stand ready to welcome us with the gifts of His eternal Kingdom; whence, even now, though unseen, He beholds every disappointment and every effort.

In the meantime, during our brief space of toil, by unexpected and strange ways, His promise finds fulfilment. He does not leave His people desolate, though they do not always or at once recognise their visitation. Not once or twice only, but as often the cleansed eye is turned to revolutions of society or to revolutions of thought, to the

[margin: VI. Luke xxi. 19. Apoc. xxi. 1.]

VI. breaking of a new day over the restless waters of life, the believer knows by an access of power, of knowledge, of love, that His words are true: *I come to you.*

VII.

THE REVELATION THROUGH ACTIVE WORK.

Ὅτε οὖν ἠρίστησαν λέγει τῷ Σίμωνι Πέτρῳ ὁ Ἰησοῦς Σίμων Ἰωάνου, ἀγαπᾷς με πλέον τούτων; λέγει αὐτῷ Ναί, κύριε, σὺ οἶδας ὅτι φιλῶ σε. λέγει αὐτῷ Βόσκε τὰ ἀρνία μου. λέγει αὐτῷ πάλιν δεύτερον Σίμων Ἰωάνου, ἀγαπᾷς με; λέγει αὐτῷ Ναί, κύριε, σὺ οἶδας ὅτι φιλῶ σε. λέγει αὐτῷ Ποίμαινε τὰ προβάτιά μου. λέγει αὐτῷ τὸ τρίτον Σίμων Ἰωάνου, φιλεῖς με; ἐλυπήθη ὁ Πέτρος ὅτι εἶπεν αὐτῷ τὸ τρίτον Φιλεῖς με; καὶ εἶπεν αὐτῷ Κύριε, πάντα σὺ οἶδας, σὺ γινώσκεις ὅτι φιλῶ σε. λέγει αὐτῷ Ἰησοῦς Βόσκε τὰ προβάτιά μου. ἀμὴν ἀμὴν λέγω σοι, ὅτε ἦς νεώτερος, ἐζώννυες σεαυτὸν καὶ περιεπάτεις ὅπου ἤθελες· ὅταν δὲ γηράσῃς, ἐκτενεῖς τὰς χεῖράς σου, καὶ ἄλλος ζώσει σε καὶ οἴσει ὅπου οὐ θέλεις. τοῦτο δὲ εἶπεν σημαίνων ποίῳ θανάτῳ δοξάσει τὸν θεόν. καὶ τοῦτο εἰπὼν λέγει αὐτῷ Ἀκολούθει μοι.

So when they had broken their fast, Jesus saith to Simon Peter, Simon, son of John, lovest thou me more than these? He saith unto him, Yea, Lord; thou knowest that I love thee. He saith unto him, Feed my lambs. He saith to him again a second time, Simon, son of John, lovest thou me? He saith unto him, Yea, Lord; thou knowest that I love thee. He saith unto him, Tend my sheep. He saith unto him the third time, Simon, son of John, lovest thou me? Peter was grieved because he said unto him the third time, Lovest thou me? And he said unto him, Lord, thou knowest all things; thou knowest that I love thee. Jesus saith unto him, Feed my sheep. Verily, verily, I say unto thee, When thou wast young, thou girdedst thyself, and walkedst whither thou wouldest: but when thou shalt be old, thou shalt stretch forth thy hands, and another shall gird thee, and carry thee whither thou wouldest not. Now this he spake, signifying by what manner of death he should glorify God. And when he had spoken this, he saith unto him, Follow me.
JOHN xxi. 15—19.

Τῇ σπουδῇ μὴ ὀκνηροί, τῷ πνεύματι ζέοντες, τῷ κυρίῳ δουλεύοντες.

In diligence not slothful: fervent in spirit; serving the Lord.

Rom. xii. 11.

THE REVELATION IN THE WORK OF LIFE:

THE SERVICE OF WORKING.

WE have seen that the Revelation of the Risen Lord by the sea of Tiberias shews in a figure the general character of the apostolic work—a work laid upon all Christians in different ways—and of the light that comes through it: how that waiting, labouring, obeying, the servants of the Lord will in due time know that He is with them by gifts of success and by gifts of refreshment. This universal lesson is illustrated in the sequel of the narrative by a portraiture of two great types of apostolic service, the service of active energy and the service of patient waiting, the service of St Peter and the service of St John, the one consummated in the martyrdom of death, the other wrought out to the end in the martyrdom of life.

In this respect the second part of the history develops what has been indicated in the first.

VII. For the characteristic differences of the two apostles, of the two forms of service, can be seen in the circumstances of the miracle. St John was the first to recognise the Lord from the fisher's boat, but St Peter was the first to join Him. It was enough for St John to know that the Lord was near, and to guard the prize which He had given, and to tarry till in due order he was carried to His feet. But St Peter could bear no delay. Even if the ship was not far from the land he must cast himself into the sea that he might by however little be sooner with the Lord. On the one side there is the clear vision which looks straight to the heart of things, the calm trust which reposes in the Divine guidance, the self-sacrifice in which self is forgotten. On the other side there is the prompt resolve which takes no count of the cost, the courageous activity which dares all things, the self-sacrifice in which self is offered. Both types of service are consecrated; and it is well that we should recognise both with equal thankfulness.

When they had broken their fast, we read, *Jesus saith to Simon Peter, Simon, son of John, lovest thou me more than these,* more that is than these thy fellow disciples, whose love is seen in their silent devotion. Every word was charged with a fulness of meaning. The name so spoken

—Simon son of John—recalled the two noblest moments in the apostle's life, the one when he was first brought to Christ, and *Jesus looked upon him and said, Thou art Simon the son of John, thou shalt be called Cephas.* The other, when after his great confession, *Jesus said unto him, Blessed art thou, Simon Bar-Jonah, for flesh and blood hath not revealed it unto thee, but my Father which is in heaven. And I also say unto thee, That thou art Peter, and upon this rock I will build my Church.* Had he then justified this name—the Rock-man? He had ventured to say on the Eve of the Passion, *If all shall be offended in Thee, I will never be offended. Lord ...I will lay down my life for Thee.* How had he fulfilled these bold promises? We can all feel that the swift retrospect thus called up must have been full of sadness. But at the same time it brought an opportunity for a humbler expression of attachment. The love of which Christ spoke was something absolute, heavenly, eternal: St Peter had not, as he had painfully learnt, reached to the pure heights of such love, but even in the depths of his sorrow and humiliation he was sure of his personal affection. He raises now no question of comparison with others. He will not even trust to his own self-knowledge. He appeals to Christ Himself as witness to his words. *Yea,*

VII.

John i.

Matt. xvi. 17.

Matt. xxvi. 33.
John xiii. 37.

Lord, thou knowest that I love Thee—love Thee, not as Thou requirest, not as I would, but with a true devotion. St Peter on this occasion had not overrated his strength, and so he was able to receive the Lord's commission; *He saith unto him, Feed my lambs.* The fisher's work was to be followed by the shepherd's work. Those who were brought within the Church were to be watched with untiring solicitude.

The first, the simplest part of the apostolic charge, is to provide Christ's little ones with that which is needed for their support; but it is not all. *He saith to him again a second time, Simon, son of John, lovest thou me?* The Lord repeats the word for 'love' which He had used before, but He no longer adds the reference to the apostle's abandoned claim, 'more than these.' So far He accepts his confession while He proves it still further. St Peter however has nothing to change, nothing to add. His answer is literally the same as before. *Yea, Lord, Thou knowest that I love Thee.* At once a new charge follows. *He saith to him, Tend*—shepherd (not simply feed)—*my sheep* (not lambs). If there are the young and the weak and the ignorant to be fed, there are also the mature and the vigorous to be guided. The shepherd must rule no less than feed. And to do this wisely and well is a harder work than the first.

Yet something more remained. The proof of St Peter was not yet completed, the office of St Peter was not yet fully set forth. *He saith unto him the third time, Simon, son of John, lovest thou Me*—and now the Lord used the apostle's own word for love—lovest thou Me, that is, as thou sayest thyself, and not as I asked before? lovest thou Me with the affection which will give up all for a friend? The form of the question could not but touch St Peter to the quick. If the three questions recalled his three denials, the language of this last must have vividly brought back to him his failure even in personal devotion at the moment of trial. *Peter was grieved because He said unto him the third time, Lovest thou me*, not merely that the question was put again, but that it was so put as to cast a doubt even on the modified love which he had professed; and the strength of his grief lay in the deep consciousness that the doubt was justified by the past. Yet even in this extremity he has a sure trust. He leaves out the affirmation which he had made before, and throws himself wholly upon Christ. *Lord*, he says, *Thou knowest all things*—Thou knowest my false confidence, my bold words, my miserable failures, my bitter tears—Thou knowest my Easter joy and my patient waiting since— *Thou knowest all things*, and, at this moment

132 *The issue of St Peter's life.*

VII. reading my heart as I cannot read it, *Thou seest that I love Thee,* love Thee even as I said. The appeal was not in vain. *Jesus saith unto him, Feed my sheep.* Feed my sheep, as He had said before, *Feed my lambs:* 'Feed' and not 'tend' or 'shepherd' only. This was the final commission; and if it is hard to guide the full-grown Christian with wise authority, it is still harder to provide in due season that which shall maintain and increase the fruitfulness of his life. But this also belongs to the shepherd's work. Every ministry of tender anxiety and gentle forethought must be rendered to the strong as well as to the weak. To do this is the highest and noblest triumph of pastoral care.

St Peter had learnt what he was to do for others: what, he might ask, would be the issue for himself. The Lord anticipated the inquiry. *Verily, verily, I say unto thee, when thou wast younger, thou girdedst thyself and walkedst whither thou wouldest: but when thou shalt be old, thou shalt stretch forth thy hands and another shall gird thee, and carry thee whither thou wouldest not.* The words could not but appear at the time dark and mysterious. So much could be seen that they told of an end of utter powerlessness, of a time when the apostle should be helpless in the hands of others, held in bondage and incapable of

The type of active service. 133

resistance. They had a deeper and more tragic meaning, which was as yet hidden; but this and much more was shadowed out in the two words which the Lord added: *When He had spoken this, He saith unto him, Follow me:* follow Me, though hereafter the spiritual eye alone will see Me: follow Me, though the way, as far as it is opened, will seem strange: follow Me, though the end, as far as this earth is concerned, will be death upon the Cross.

The narrative read thus simply and literally presents, in a most impressive shape, the foundation, the character, the issue of the active service of Christ. The foundation is love: the character is considerate thoughtfulness: the issue is self-surrender. The lessons are, no doubt, in the fullest sense for those to whom the oversight of Christ's flock is committed; but in a most true sense they are for all to whom God has given energy and strength, the power of action and the zeal for movement.

Love, love to Christ, which is the one sure spring of love to men, is the foundation of service. It is the first condition of the divine charge, and the second, and the third. It is the spirit of the new Covenant which burns not to consume but to purify. In the prospect of work for others or for ourselves we can always hear the one question in the stillness of our souls, 'Lovest thou me?' Love may not, cannot, be attained in its fulness at once; but the Person of Christ, if indeed we see Him as He is presented to us in the Gospels, will kindle that direct affection out of which it comes. If our hearts were less dull we could not study the changing scenes of His unchanging love, or attempt to describe them to others, without answering the silent appeal which they make to us in St Peter's words: *Lord, Thou knowest that I love Thee;* yes, and still more, these which are Thine and not mine, these who fall under my influence in the various relations of life, for Thy sake.

The foundation of service is love, the rule of service is thoughtfulness. If we are to do Christ's work we must consider more patiently than we commonly do the requirements of those whom we have to serve. There is not one method, one voice for all. Here there is need of the tenderest simplicity: there of the wisest authority: there of the ripest result of long reflection. The true teacher, and as Christians we are all teachers, will temper the application of his experience with anxious care. It is to our great loss, we must all sadly confess, that we forget now the lambs and now the sheep of Christ's flock. The former too

thoughtfulness and self-surrender.

often perish through our grievous fault for lack of food, and the latter for lack of guidance.

The service which rests on love and is ruled by thoughtfulness issues in self-surrender. The impetuous vigour of early days loses its self-confidence without losing its strength. The servant who has wrought much for his Lord has learned to trust Him. His joy is when no choice is left: his freedom is to give up his own desire. The sentence which sounds at first like a sentence of hopeless bondage receives a new meaning. As the outward man is confined more and more closely, the inward man, by God's grace, grows to fuller proportions. And he to whom Christ speaks can interpret as a last promise of conformity to Himself the solemn words: *Another shall gird thee, and carry thee whither thou wouldest not.*

The tradition of the death of St Peter offers a striking commentary on the thoughts which are thus suggested. On the eve of his martyrdom, as it is said, the friends of the apostle obtained the means for his escape. They pleaded the desolation of the Church. He may have remembered his deliverance by the angel from Herod's prison. And so he yielded to their prayers. The city was now left and he was hastening along the Appian way, when the Lord met him. Lord, whither goest thou? was his one eager question; and the reply followed, 'I go to Rome to be crucified again 'for thee.'

Next morning the prisoner was found by the keepers in his cell; and St Peter gained the fulfilment of the Lord's words and followed Him even to the cross.

The tradition may be only a thought clothed in an outward dress, but it gathers up with singular power and beauty the sum of what has been said. If that Divine Figure rises before us in the crisis of our trial, service will be transfigured by the glory of Him who came not to be ministered unto, but to minister. So looking to Christ we shall come to understand little by little the meaning of His command, sufficient alone to move, to guide, to support, *Follow Me*.

VIII.

THE REVELATION THROUGH PATIENT WAITING.

Ἐπιστραφεὶς ὁ Πέτρος βλέπει τὸν μαθητὴν ὃν ἠγάπα ὁ Ἰησοῦς ἀκολουθοῦντα, ὃς καὶ ἀνέπεσεν ἐν τῷ δείπνῳ ἐπὶ τὸ στῆθος αὐτοῦ καὶ εἶπεν Κύριε, τίς ἐστιν ὁ παραδιδούς σε; τοῦτον οὖν ἰδὼν ὁ Πέτρος λέγει τῷ Ἰησοῦ Κύριε, οὗτος δὲ τί; λέγει αὐτῷ ὁ Ἰησοῦς Ἐὰν αὐτὸν θέλω μένειν ἕως ἔρχομαι, τί πρὸς σέ; σύ μοι ἀκολούθει. Ἐξῆλθεν οὖν οὗτος ὁ λόγος εἰς τοὺς ἀδελφοὺς ὅτι ὁ μαθητὴς ἐκεῖνος οὐκ ἀποθνήσκει. οὐκ εἶπεν δὲ αὐτῷ ὁ Ἰησοῦς ὅτι οὐκ ἀποθνήσκει, ἀλλ' Ἐὰν αὐτὸν θέλω μένειν ἕως ἔρχομαι, τί πρὸς σέ;

Peter, turning about, seeth the disciple whom Jesus loved following; which also leaned back on his breast at the supper, and said, Lord, who is he that betrayeth thee? Peter therefore seeing him saith to Jesus, Lord, and what shall this man do? Jesus saith unto him, If I will that he tarry till I come, what is that to thee? follow thou me. This saying therefore went forth among the brethren, that that disciple should not die: yet Jesus said not unto him, that he should not die; but, If I will that he tarry till I come, what is that *to thee?*

JOHN xxi. 20—23.

Τῇ ἐλπίδι χαίροντες, τῇ θλίψει ὑπομένοντες, τῇ προσευχῇ προσκαρτεροῦντες.

Rejoicing in hope; patient in tribulation; continuing stedfastly in prayer.

Rom. xii. 12.

THE REVELATION IN THE WORK OF LIFE:

THE SERVICE OF WAITING.

THE last record of St John's Gospel brings VIII.
before us a singular phase of early Christian
thought and of early Christian error. There was,
as we know from the Epistles, a widely-spread
belief in the apostolic age that the Lord would
return in glory before the first generation of believers had passed away, to exercise His power as
Judge and King over the world. The belief was
true in its spiritual essence, but false so far as it was
clothed by human enthusiasm in a material shape.
The Lord did come at the time expected. He did
execute vengeance and assume sovereignty, but
otherwise than men had dreamt. So it always
has been: so, we must conclude, it always will be.
The comings of the Lord are not such events as
we look for. Perhaps they are unregarded by
those who witness them; but they are not therefore less real or less momentous.

In this respect the fulfilment of the words of
Christ, in which He said that some who heard

VIII. Him should 'not taste of death till the Son of 'man came in His kingdom,' may help us to interpret other crises.

We can now perhaps with some difficulty understand in part what the destruction of the Holy City—that shaking not of the earth only but also of heaven—was for those who had been reared in Judaism; how that terrible catastrophe closed a period in the divine revelation; how the Christian Church became thenceforth the sole appointed seat of God's Presence with men: how a society, universal in its teaching and constitution and range, was substituted finally and for ever in place of that which had prepared the way for it. We can, I say, see this now, and acknowledge the coming of the Lord, when distant objects appear in their true proportions—and it will be well if the lesson helps us to know the day of our visitation—but the first Christians, in the confusion of their conflicts, could not see it. They had decided in what way Christ should come, and so looked for the establishment of their own belief and not of His promise. When St John alone remained of the twelve, they still clung to their fancies, and they found in words addressed to him a confirmation of their error. *The saying went forth among the brethren that that disciple should not die.* He at least, so they supposed, would

Following and waiting. 143

remain alive on earth to meet the returning Lord; and so strong was the conviction that even when the apostle was laid to rest, it was reported for centuries that the dust above his grave was gently moved by the breathing of the saint beneath not dead but sleeping. St John had heard of the wrong use which had been made of Christ's words and in the passage before us he corrects it. The mode of correction is remarkable. For he corrects the popular error not by any argument, not by any fresh interpretation, not by any decision of authority, but simply by repeating the actual phrase which was spoken. It might be that the Lord had some purpose with regard to him which he could not anticipate. At any rate it was not his part to determine beforehand all that He must mean. The whole Truth was in His own language. To keep to that faithfully and patiently was to avoid error. *Jesus said not unto him that he should not die, but If I will that he tarry till I come, what is that to thee?*

As the Evangelist recalled the words he laid open the secret of his own life. For when we look back we can perceive how the two mysterious sentences spoken on that early morning by the sea of Tiberias, 'Follow thou me,' 'If I will that 'he tarry till I come,' describe the destinies of the two representative apostles, of whom they were spoken; how they were fulfilled more than in the letter; how they mark two types of service which must always be rendered, if the Church is to reconcile order with progress, the service of working and the service of waiting, the service of action and the service of thought, the service of outward effort fashioned after the likeness of Christ's Passion and the service of inward meditation directed to the vision of Christ's coming, the one, as has been well said, symbolised in the promise of the Cross, and the other in the promise of the Apocalypse.

We have already touched upon the service of St Peter. We have yet to consider the service of St John. And there is something at first sight most strange in the place which St John occupies in the apostolic records. He appears three times only in the history after the Ascension, and then simply by the side of St Peter. His brother James was taken as the first martyr among the apostles, but he was himself untouched. St Peter declared the reception of the Gentiles to the apostles and brethren at Jerusalem, but he is silent. St Paul recounted his work, but he is silent still. He had received for his charge the mother of the Lord, and perhaps he remained apart in his Galilæan home pondering over the mysteries which that charge brought nearer to him, and finding little

tarrying till the Lord came.

by little the full meaning of that which he had seen and handled, as the Truth was partially embodied by men:

"What first were guessed as points he then knew stars."

However it was, for thirty years or more he remained in silence. Some might have thought that he had been wrongly named, or admitted in vain to the closest fellowship with his Master. But when the time was fully come the Apocalypse proved that he had not ceased to be a son of Thunder; and yet later his Gospel shewed in every line the insight of the disciple whom Jesus loved. He tarried till the Lord came, and then he was prepared to do the work which could not have been done before, and (we may dare to say) which could not have been done without such a preparation.

What this work was which was thus slowly matured we can in some way imagine by removing the Fourth Gospel from the New Testament and then counting our loss. Without it we might have asked, half sadly, as men have asked, whether our faith was not fashioned by St Paul, whether there was indeed any anticipation in the Lord's own words of the issues of His work, whether He so spoke as to meet the questionings of a later age. With it we have for our heritage

VIII.

John viii.
12; xiv. 20;
xi. 25.

1 John i. 4.

what St John found at last in the Lord's teaching through the discipline of his own experience, thoughts of truth and unity and life which satisfy the heart and transcend all speculation, thoughts made facts in the Person of Christ. *I am the light of the world: I am in my Father and ye in Me and I in you: I am the Resurrection and the Life.* These divine utterances St John was enabled to preserve for our instruction and comfort as the Spirit called back to him in the silent watches of his waiting what the Lord had said. These revelations speak through all time with a voice of strength for the feeble and a voice of peace for the distracted. The disciple whom Jesus loved tarried till his Master came; and when He came he was ready to present Him to the world in His glory that the joy of believers might be fulfilled. In such a way St John's work of waiting was consummated. The long silence was followed by the proclamation of the Truth which had been silently realised. Not one hour of that term of stillness, we can feel, was lost. And as we look with thankfulness to the results of St John's labour of patience we may find a lesson for ourselves. We can all, I fancy, sympathise with the passionate zeal and stirring energy of St Peter. There is something congenial to the spirit of our times in his bold movement and impetuous

its proper place.

courage. If our hearts are touched, we are eager to give instant expression to our emotions. We estimate the value of a cause by its immediate effect. We claim that convictions should at once vindicate their reality by conquest. If one stands by us with eye and soul fixed, as we are sure, on the object of our adoration, calmly and silently, we are inclined to ask with an impatient curiosity, strong it may be, like St Peter, in the consciousness of our own call to action, *Lord and what shall this man do?* We are tempted perhaps to make the prayer of Martha our own: 'Lord, dost thou not care that he hath left us alone? Bid him that he help us.' In such a case it will be our happiness to hear the Lord's answer to St Peter, and to welcome with meekness the Lord's reproof: *If I will that he tarry till I come, what is that to thee? Follow thou Me.* Each man has his own work to do: this one to serve, that one to sit at the Lord's feet: this one to follow, that one to wait. The disposition rests with Him who claims a sovereign power over the destiny of His disciples, and regards the well-being of all. And just that type of devout ministry is most needful which is most foreign to the prevailing bent.

No one who feels the sorrows of the age would wish to disparage the new earnestness which impels men at present even to undisciplined and

VIII.
Num. xi. 29.

self-willed efforts for Christ's sake. We say rather: *Would God that all the Lord's people were prophets.* But there are dangers in this tumult of reawakened life. Patient watching is too often treated at present with suspicion and stigmatized as lukewarmness. Judgments on the deepest mysteries are received without reflection and repeated without inquiry. Humility is interpreted as a confession of weakness and reserve is condemned as a cloke for doubt. Nothing brings such sad misgivings as this hasty, intolerant temper, peculiar to no one party or class, which is characteristic of the age. If, as we cannot but believe, the Lord is even now coming to His Church, we shall be ill prepared to meet Him unless there be some among us tarrying for Him in self-concentration and silence, looking to Him and lost in Him: men who dare to wait and stand outside the battle in which as yet they have no part, who dare to hold their peace till the meaning of the Spirit is clear, who dare to refuse to accept the most venerable human gloss as the full and final exponent of the Divine Word, which still they may be themselves quite unable to interpret.

Those who have studied the life of the Church have often remarked that the history of the apostolic age has been reproduced on a large scale in the history of Christendom. St Peter, St Paul and St John occupy in succession the principal VIII. place in the first century, each carrying forward in due measure the work to which he ministered. So, it is said, we may see the likeness of St Peter in the Church of the Middle Ages, and the likeness of St Paul in the Churches of the Reformation. There remains then, such is the conclusion, yet one more type of the Christian society to be realised in the world, which shall bear the likeness of St John. Whether this be so or not, and many things combine to force upon us the belief that we are approaching some great change of religious life, the record before us lays down the one sure rule for our guidance, whatever our special duty may be. If we are called to action, Christ is the Way: if we are called to thought, Christ is the Truth. To those His command is 'Follow Me:' to these 'Tarry till I come.' Working or waiting our steps will be turned to Him: our souls will hang on Him.

And waiting, as we must recognise and remember, is a sacrifice of self, a real martyrdom no less than working. St John by his long life, as truly as St James by his early death, drank of the Lord's Cup and shared in the Lord's Baptism according to His own words. To win the soul in patience, to bear the trial of delays, to watch for the dawn through the chill hours which precede

Mark x. 39.

it, to keep fresh and unsullied the great hope that Christ will come, without presuming to decide the fashion of His Coming, is a witness to the powers of the unseen world, which the Spirit of God alone can make possible. It is a witness which we need at present. We ourselves, or some among us, may be called to give it: at least we are called to pray that it may be given. For it seems to offer the divine antidote to the wilfulness and dogmatism which threaten to paralyse our strength. Our differences will be seen in their proper dimensions if we stand as men looking for the Return of their Lord, if Advent awakens a faith and not only a memory. We shall learn to tolerate the imperfections of human language if we strive to rise through words to Him whom they half veil and half reveal, perfect God and perfect man, who was born and died and rose again for us. We shall see him even now in the consciousness of His Presence, as Life and Light and Love, working or waiting, as it may be, if we bear about with us the vital conviction that He will come, how we know not, when we know not; come once more to claim as His own every fragment of true thought and right action; come to welcome as the blessed of His Father every one who has served Him in the disguise of the weak and the needy and the sorrowful.

IX.

THE REVELATION OF THE KINGDOM.

Οἱ δὲ ἕνδεκα μαθηταὶ ἐπορεύθησαν εἰς τὴν Γαλιλαίαν εἰς τὸ ὄρος οὗ ἐτάξατο αὐτοῖς ὁ Ἰησοῦς, καὶ ἰδόντες αὐτὸν προσεκεύνησαν, οἱ δὲ ἐδίστασαν. καὶ προσελθὼν ὁ Ἰησοῦς ἐλάλησεν αὐτοῖς λέγων Ἐδόθη μοι πᾶσα ἐξουσία ἐν οὐρανῷ καὶ ἐπὶ [τῆς] γῆς· πορευθέντες οὖν μαθητεύσατε πάντα τὰ ἔθνη, βαπτίζοντες αὐτοὺς εἰς τὸ ὄνομα τοῦ πατρὸς καὶ τοῦ υἱοῦ καὶ τοῦ ἁγίου πνεύματος, διδάσκοντες αὐτοὺς τηρεῖν πάντα ὅσα ἐνετειλάμην ὑμῖν· καὶ ἰδοὺ ἐγὼ μεθ᾿ ὑμῶν εἰμι πάσας τὰς ἡμέρας ἕως τῆς συντελείας τοῦ αἰῶνος.

But the eleven disciples went into Galilee, unto the mountain where Jesus had appointed them. And when they saw him, they worshipped him: but some doubted. And Jesus came to them and spake unto them, saying, All authority hath been given unto me in heaven and on earth. Go ye therefore, and make disciples of all the nations, baptizing them into the name of the Father and of the Son and of the Holy Ghost: teaching them to observe all things whatsoever I commanded you: and lo, I am with you alway, even unto the end of the world.

MATT. xxviii. 16—20.

Ἐγένετο ἡ βασιλεία τοῦ κόσμου τοῦ κυρίου ἡμῶν καὶ τοῦ χριστοῦ αὐτοῦ, καὶ βασιλεύσει εἰς τοὺς αἰῶνας τῶν αἰώνων.

The kingdom of the world is become the kingdom of our Lord, and of his Christ: and he shall reign for ever and ever.

APOC. xi. 15.

THE REVELATION OF THE KINGDOM.

THE appearance of the Risen Lord to the disciples in Galilee related by St Matthew, is in many respects different from those which we have already considered. The record is distinctively that of an appearance in Royal Majesty, and therefore it fitly closes the first Gospel, the Gospel of 'the Christ,' the King. The end of the narrative answers to the beginning. The adoration of the Wise Men finds its counterpart and completion in the adoration of the disciples. The promise of the prophetic name Immanuel— God with us—is fulfilled in the Lord's own assurance: *I am with you all the days unto the end of the world.*

The scene and the circumstances of the Appearance correspond with its character. The manifestation is no longer in the upper chamber where the disciples are assembled in fear with closed doors; nor yet by the shore of the restless sea on which they have toiled in vain. It is not a surprise to men lost in sorrow or doubt, as to Mary Magdalene and the two disciples. It is not a resolution of individual difficulties as to St Thomas. It is not a revelation half veiled under mysterious symbols, as by the Sea of Tiberias. Time and place and persons appear to have been fixed beforehand. The Lord was seen by the disciples on *the mountain where He had appointed them.* It is not possible indeed to fix the exact locality, but it was evidently chosen by Him with a significant purpose. Just as He had gone up into 'the mountain' when He solemnly commenced His teaching of the multitudes: just as He had continued all night in prayer to God upon 'the mountain' before He commissioned the twelve apostles; just as He chose 'the mountain' as the spot where St Peter and St James and St John were allowed to catch a passing glimpse of His glory: so here He stands upon 'the mountain' when He declares the extent, the method, the duration of His sovereignty.

If we had St Matthew's narrative alone we should probably suppose that none but the eleven were present to receive the Lord's charge. In that case the reference to 'some who doubted' would be almost unintelligible. But the brief summary of St Paul leads us to conclude that it

Matt. v. 1.

Luke vi. 12.

Luke ix. 28.

was on this occasion that the Lord *appeared to above five hundred brethren at once.* We can then rightly picture to ourselves the whole congregation of believers now gathered once more round their Divine Master at a spot hallowed by earlier memories. They had received at Jerusalem the great spiritual commission, and now they were to learn how it should be executed. The record is evidently brought into the narrowest compass. At the same time every word in which the charge is given bears the impress of Divine sovereignty. No language can go beyond the terms in which the Lord sets forth His absolute power. *All authority,* He says, *is given unto Me in heaven and on earth.* To feel the force of such a sentence, we must remember that He who spoke had been crucified not many days before amidst the mockery of His enemies and the despair of His followers. But now He lays open the eternal issues of that death. Not earth only but heaven is subject to His dominion. All created being has been brought under His sway—angels, and men, and nature. In Him whatever before was most widely separated has found a final unity. The power *is given* Him. It represents the love of the Father no less than the victory of the Son. It is the pledge of the triumph of the Father's will; and His will is the salvation of men. *Go there-*

IX.

1 Cor. xv. 6.

fore, the Lord continues, 'therefore,' because you can now see the right which I have to command, because you can now find your own weakness perfected in my strength, because unseen powers are leagued on your side, *go and make disciples of all the nations.* This is the end of My kingship, to win for Myself willing subjects: this is the aim of your service, to unite mankind in loyal allegiance to the truth.

Make disciples of all the nations. The grandeur of the charge and the apparent inadequacy of the instruments are alike surprising. Up to this time the ministry of the disciples was restricted to *the lost sheep of the house of Israel*: now Israel is reckoned among the nations. The Risen Christ claims for Himself not one people but all. His kingdom is thus from the beginning revealed in its utmost range. The fulness of time has come. All things are ready.

If those to whom He spoke had been told to measure their own resources, to look first to the influences of authority or place or wisdom for victory, they might well have despaired. But the words that follow set aside such a misgiving. They had simply a message to proclaim and the blessing of a heavenly communion to offer. Here as always the grace of God comes first, which makes the later work of man possible. *Make disciples of all the nations*, the Lord says, *baptizing them into*—not '*in*'—*the name of the Father, and of the Son, and of the Holy Spirit*. The beginning of discipleship lies in the reception of a Divine gift by those who are willing to accept it. The power through which we can render peaceful obedience cannot originate in ourselves. But the new Sacrament of Baptism, now first instituted, establishes the connexion through which the currents of the spiritual life flow, if I may so speak, naturally. It forces us to look away from ourselves for the strength which we need. It concentrates our thoughts on God's loving purpose. It offers us—sense-bound as we are—a historical pledge that He on His part will most surely accomplish what He has begun. It gives us that point of support whereby we are enabled to move the world.

The more we reflect on that brief sentence, *baptizing them into the name of the Father, and of the Son, and of the Holy Ghost*, the more we shall feel with a living conviction that it includes the foundation of all our confidence, the sum of all our creed. The Divine title is declared to be a 'name' and not 'names,' that we may hold firmly to the Unity of the Divine Essence, while each Person is separately mentioned that we may feel our manifold dependence upon the one God.

IX. Thus the name of the most Holy Trinity expresses all that has been made known to us of the relation of the Godhead to ourselves, as we are created, redeemed, sanctified. And to be 'baptized into this name' is to be brought in God's own way into fellowship with Him Who has been so revealed. Just as in all other things, the years that follow will shew how the privilege is used or wasted. So far as we become fellow-workers with God all later life is the gradual realisation by faith of the blessing thus given in its potential germ, the gradual realisation by thought of the Truth thus shadowed out, the fashioning of the divine image in which we were made to the divine likeness unto which we were destined.

For the work of 'discipling the nations' is not completed when allegiance is pledged and union formed. Teaching follows baptizing. Little by little to the end of the individual life and to the end of all time the words of Christ are apprehended in their fulness. The ripest believer has not reached the limit to which he can attain. The latest age has not exhausted the meaning of what was once said. All experience shews us something more in that which we have long possessed. All progress enlarges our prospect of the marvels of the Divine counsel. We must keep every sense open, every faculty exercised if we are to do our part in furthering the spiritual conquest of the world. In one sense all has been done: in another sense all remains to do. No addition can be made to God's love: no addition can be made to Christ's words. But we on our side can respond to the love more warmly; we can enter into the words more deeply; and this we must do, if we are not to stand still while all around is moving. For to stand is to die.

Thus we are brought to the promise which makes the universal mission-work of the Christian, ever apprehended in the course of the ages as vaster and more intense, practicable for every one of us. The Christian is not alone even if he seems to be alone. *Lo I am with you,* Christ said, *all the days*—all the days—*unto the end of the world.* And this peculiar phrase in which the promise is expressed in the original turns our thoughts to the manifold vicissitudes of fortune in which the Lord is still present with His people. He does not say simply 'always,' as of a uniform duration, but 'all the days,' as if He would take account of the changing aspects of storm and sunshine, of light and darkness, which chequer our course. Such alternations of joy and mourning, of success and failure, belong to the very conditions of our existence. We cannot even imagine a state of unbroken calm. As we are constituted at present conflict and effort are a necessity, and so too, as the consequences of sin, are defeat and sorrow. Yet even so defeat will lose its bitterness, and sorrow will lose its sting, if we know that Christ is with us 'all the days;' 'all the days,' even when we are most tempted to forget Him in the brightness of human joy, or to doubt His nearness in the solitude of our bereavement.

The sense of this abiding Presence of God in Christ both with the Church at large and with individual believers is that which we need sorely in this time of restlessness and debate. Nothing else, so far as I see, appears to be equally fitted to bring patience, and with patience peace. There is something deadening in the strife of words. The silence which follows controversy is very commonly the sign of exhaustion and not of rest. We require to be taken up out of our little circle of strifes and questionings, as it were into a mountain, that so we may regard our King in His glory as He has there revealed Himself. It is not by narrowing our vision or our sympathy, by fixing our eyes simply on that which is congenial to our feelings, by excluding from our interest whole regions of Christendom, that we can gain

abiding Presence. 163

the repose of faith. We must dare to look on the broad and chequered aspect of life. We must dare to confess that Christ calls all the nations to His service through us; and no less to maintain that He is everywhere with the two or three gathered together in His name.

To do this is not easy; and to the last, as we strive to do it more faithfully, we shall find ourselves face to face with mysteries which we cannot solve. But we shall at least gain this, that we shall learn a little more of the vastness of God's sovereignty; and looking over the course of its gradual establishment we shall perceive how He uses unexpected means to fulfil His will. We shall become sure that His cause does go forward. If in a moment of trial some pitiless power compels us to confess that appearances, tradition, authority are against us, we shall answer in our souls 'and yet it moves.' And if we cannot obtain more than partial knowledge we shall secure perfect trust. And this will send us back cheered and strengthened to our proper work. For the conviction that God works in other ways than our's will not make our own calling, His voice to us, less distinct or less imperative. The belief that He is with others will not shake our belief that He is with us. Nay rather, the power of His Presence among us will be multiplied when we know that we are not alone, and that while human infirmity and wilfulness may cloud His glory, yet they cannot banish His love.

At the same time this assurance of Christ's Presence 'all the days,' which blesses effort, does not dispense with effort. It is not enough to know that He is with us: we must use His help. He gives the promise after the command, *Go and make disciples of all the nations......and lo I am with you all the days*. There is work to be done as there is a blessing to be secured. The recognition of His presence is the preparation for His coming. But if we would hasten His coming we must feel that He is indeed with us.

It is a natural but false feeling which leads us to think that at some other time God was nearer to the world than He is now; that His voice was clearer and more intelligible; that His government was more direct and uniform. He is, if only we will look, still among us, speaking to those who listen through the manifold discoveries of the age, guiding even our fierce and selfish conflicts so as to minister to His purpose. And we ourselves consciously or unconsciously are serving Him. He uses us if we do not bring ourselves to Him a willing sacrifice. We cannot doubt this; and we cannot fail to see what a different world it would be, if still remaining faithful to our personal convictions, abandoning nothing of the Truth which has been made known to us, yielding no fragment of the position which has been committed to our keeping, we could all agree in holding as a living fact the reality of Christ's universal Presence: in looking to Him in the execution of our designs, as using them for some larger end; in making Him the witness of our actions, as tributary to a counsel beyond our thoughts. Nothing less than this is the scope of His words: *I am with you all the days, unto the end of the world.* I—perfect God and perfect Man—able to help and to sympathise to the uttermost—I am with you. The promise has never been revoked. It has been forgotten: it has been practically denied: but it stands written still to reveal the heaven which lies about us, the powers which are ready for our hands.

Καὶ εἶπεν αὐτοῖς Πορευθέντες εἰς τὸν κόσμον ἄπαντα κηρύξατε τὸ εὐαγγέλιον πάσῃ τῇ κτίσει. ὁ πιστεύσας καὶ βαπτισθεὶς σωθήσεται, ὁ δὲ ἀπιστήσας κατακριθήσεται. σημεῖα δὲ τοῖς πιστεύσασιν ἀκολουθήσει ταῦτα, ἐν τῷ ὀνόματί μου δαιμόνια ἐκβαλοῦσιν, γλώσσαις λαλήσουσιν, [καὶ ἐν ταῖς χερσὶν] ὄφεις ἀροῦσιν κἂν θανάσιμόν τι πίωσιν οὐ μὴ αὐτοὺς βλάψῃ, ἐπὶ ἀρρώστους χεῖρας ἐπιθήσουσιν καὶ καλῶς ἕξουσιν.

Εἶπεν δὲ πρὸς αὐτούς Οὗτοι οἱ λόγοι μου οὓς ἐλάλησα πρὸς ὑμᾶς ἔτι ὢν σὺν ὑμῖν, ὅτι δεῖ πληρωθῆναι πάντα τὰ γεγραμμένα ἐν τῷ νόμῳ Μωυσέως καὶ τοῖς προφήταις καὶ Ψαλμοῖς περὶ ἐμοῦ. τότε διήνοιξεν αὐτῶν τὸν νοῦν τοῦ συνιέναι τὰς γραφάς, καὶ εἶπεν αὐτοῖς ὅτι οὕτως γέγραπται παθεῖν τὸν χριστὸν καὶ ἀναστῆναι ἐκ νεκρῶν τῇ τρίτῃ ἡμέρᾳ, καὶ κηρυχθῆναι ἐπὶ τῷ ὀνόματι αὐτοῦ μετάνοιαν εἰς ἄφεσιν ἁμαρτιῶν εἰς πάντα τὰ ἔθνη,—ἀρξάμενοι ἀπὸ Ἱερουσαλήμ· ὑμεῖς μάρτυρες τούτων. καὶ ἰδοὺ ἐγὼ ἐξαποστέλλω τὴν ἐπαγγελίαν τοῦ πατρός μου ἐφ' ὑμᾶς· ὑμεῖς δὲ καθίσατε ἐν τῇ πόλει ἕως οὗ ἐνδύσησθε ἐξ ὕψους δύναμιν.

And he said unto them, Go ye into all the world, and preach the gospel to the whole creation. He that believeth and is baptized shall be saved; but he that disbelieveth shall be condemned. And these signs shall follow them that believe: in my name shall they cast out devils; they shall speak with new tongues; they shall take up serpents, and if they drink any deadly thing, it shall in no wise hurt them; they shall lay hands on the sick, and they shall recover.
[MARK] xvi. 15—18.

And he said unto them, These are my words which I spake unto you, while I was yet with you, how that all things must needs be fulfilled, which are written in the law of Moses, and the prophets, and the psalms, concerning me. Then opened he their mind, that they might understand the scriptures; and he said unto them, Thus it is written, that the Christ should suffer, and rise again from the dead the third day; and that repentance and ,remission of sins should be preached in his name unto all the nations, beginning from Jerusalem. Ye are witnesses of these things. And behold, I send forth the promise of my Father upon you: but tarry ye in the city, until ye be clothed with power from on high.
LUKE xxiv. 44—49.

NOTE.

THE record of St Matthew is obviously a brief summary of the Lord's words. The fulness and comprehensiveness of the triple charge compressed into a few lines, leads irresistibly to the conclusion that the Evangelist has been guided to give the substance of what was unfolded at length. At the same time I see no reason to suppose that the summary does not represent what was said on a particular occasion. While it is most true that the three verses contain in brief the sum of what has been preserved of the Lord's teaching after the Resurrection, it is in itself likely that He should on 'the mountain' in Galilee have so gathered up the lessons which He had elsewhere given in detail.

The short record in the appendix to St Mark's Gospel is in all probability a supplementary account of the appearance which St Matthew has described. It is added to the narrative of what happened on the first Easter Day, but quite loosely without any definite connexion. In each particular the words in this later narrative contain, as it were, explanatory comments. The experience of the first preachers gave definiteness to the conceptions of the Lord's presence and power.

The paragraph in St Luke (xxiv. 44—49), on the other hand, which follows the account of the appearance to the eleven and them that were with them, seems to include words which belong to the Easter Evening as well as to later occasions (comp. John xii. 44—50).

A cursory reading of St Luke's narrative, if it were taken alone, and the same remark applies to the appendix to St Mark, might lead to the conclusion that all the words of the Lord which he has recorded were spoken on Easter Evening, and were followed immediately by the Ascension. But such an interpretation is in no way required by the exact language of the Evangelist, whose words are perfectly consistent with the fuller record in the book of the Acts.

X.

DEPARTURE IN BLESSING.

Ἐξήγαγεν δὲ αὐτοὺς ἕως πρὸς Βηθανίαν, καὶ ἐπάρας τὰς χεῖρας αὐτοῦ εὐλόγησεν αὐτούς. καὶ ἐγένετο ἐν τῷ εὐλογεῖν αὐτὸν αὐτοὺς διέστη ἀπ' αὐτῶν [καὶ ἀνεφέρετο εἰς τὸν οὐρανόν]· καὶ αὐτοὶ [προσκυνήσαντες αὐτὸν] ὑπέστρεψαν εἰς Ἰερουσαλὴμ μετὰ χαρᾶς μεγάλης, καὶ ἦσαν διὰ παντὸς ἐν τῷ ἱερῷ εὐλογοῦντες τὸν θεόν.

Οἱ μὲν οὖν συνελθόντες ἠρώτων αὐτὸν λέγοντες Κύριε, εἰ ἐν τῷ χρόνῳ τούτῳ ἀποκαθιστάνεις τὴν βασιλείαν τῷ Ἰσραήλ; εἶπεν πρὸς αὐτοὺς Οὐχ ὑμῶν ἐστιν γνῶναι χρόνους ἢ καιροὺς οὓς ὁ πατὴρ ἔθετο ἐν τῇ ἰδίᾳ ἐξουσίᾳ, ἀλλὰ λήμψεσθε δύναμιν ἐπελθόντος τοῦ ἁγίου πνεύματος ἐφ' ὑμᾶς, καὶ ἔσεσθέ μου μάρτυρες ἔν τε Ἰερουσαλὴμ καὶ [ἐν] πάσῃ τῇ Ἰουδαίᾳ καὶ Σαμαρίᾳ καὶ ἕως ἐσχάτου τῆς γῆς. καὶ ταῦτα εἰπὼν βλεπόντων αὐτῶν ἐπήρθη, καὶ νεφέλη ὑπέλαβεν αὐτὸν ἀπὸ τῶν ὀφθαλμῶν αὐτῶν. καὶ ὡς ἀτενίζοντες ἦσαν εἰς τὸν οὐρανὸν πορευομένου αὐτοῦ, καὶ ἰδοὺ ἄνδρες δύο παριστήκεισαν αὐτοῖς ἐν ἐσθήσεσι λευκαῖς, οἳ καὶ εἶπαν Ἄνδρες Γαλιλαῖοι, τί ἑστήκατε βλέποντες εἰς τὸν οὐρανόν; οὗτος ὁ Ἰησοῦς ὁ ἀναλημφθεὶς ἀφ' ὑμῶν εἰς τὸν οὐρανὸν οὕτως ἐλεύσεται ὃν τρόπον ἐθεάσασθε αὐτὸν πορευόμενον εἰς τὸν οὐρανόν.

Ὁ μὲν οὖν κύριος [Ἰησοῦς] μετὰ τὸ λαλῆσαι αὐτοῖς ἀνελήμφθη εἰς τὸν οὐρανὸν καὶ ἐκάθισεν ἐκ δεξιῶν τοῦ θεοῦ. ἐκεῖνοι δὲ ἐξελθόντες ἐκήρυξαν πανταχοῦ, τοῦ κυρίου συνεργοῦντος καὶ τὸν λόγον βεβαιοῦντος διὰ τῶν ἐπακολουθούντων σημείων.

And he led them out until they were over against Bethany: and he lifted up his hands, and blessed them. And it came to pass, while he blessed them, he parted from them, and was carried up into heaven. And they worshipped him, and returned to Jerusalem with great joy: and were continually in the temple, blessing God.

LUKE xxiv. 50—53.

They therefore, when they were come together, asked him, saying, Lord, dost thou at this time restore the kingdom to Israel? And he said unto them, It is not for you to know times or seasons, which the Father hath set within his own authority. But ye shall receive power, when the Holy Ghost is come upon you: and ye shall be my witnesses both in Jerusalem, and in all Judæa and Samaria, and unto the uttermost part of the earth. And when he had said these things, as they were looking, he was taken up; and a cloud received him out of their sight. And while they were looking stedfastly into heaven as he went, behold, two men stood by them in white apparel; which also said, Ye men of Galilee, why stand ye looking into heaven? this Jesus, which was received up from you into heaven, shall so come in like manner as ye beheld him going into heaven.

ACTS i. 6—11.

So then the Lord Jesus, after he had spoken unto them, was received up into heaven, and sat down at the right hand of God. And they went forth, and preached everywhere, the Lord working with them, and confirming the word by the signs that followed. Amen.

[MARK] xvi. 19, f.

ἐγὼ τὴν ἀλήθειαν λέγω ὑμῖν, συμφέρει ὑμῖν ἵνα ἐγὼ ἀπέλθω.

I tell you the truth: It is expedient for you that I go away.

JOHN xvi. 7.

DEPARTURE IN BLESSING.

WE have already considered the various records in which details of the appearances of the Risen Lord have been preserved for us. We have sought to appreciate the characteristic scenes in which He brought personal conviction to disciples and laid open before them the fulness and the power of their social work. We have now to notice the close, the necessary close, to this form of teaching. Such a revelation as that whereby, as we read in the Acts, *Jesus...... shewed Himself alive after His Passion by many proofs appearing......by the space of forty days ......*, was necessarily preparatory and transitional. In this respect the length of time through which it was continued was not without significance. The space of forty days is always in Scripture a period of solemn waiting followed by issues of momentous interest. When the hope of the world was sheltered by the ark there was rain on the earth for forty days and forty nights.

x.

Acts i. 3.

x. When the people had been rescued from Egypt Moses was forty days on the Mount before he received the Law. For forty days the spies examined the land of Canaan, the image of our heavenly country. For forty days Elijah tarried in Horeb before he obtained the revelation of God. For so long repentance was offered to the Ninevites; for so long Ezekiel announced the typical punishment of God's people. Only once again the same period is mentioned in the Bible, where it is written that the Lord fasted in the wilderness for forty days before He began to proclaim glad tidings to the world. So it was that Christ's ministry ended as it began. The same mysterious, measured, space in each case separated and united the old and the new.

But while there is this correspondence between the opening and the close of the Lord's ministry, it is correspondence and not identity. The forty days after the Baptism, the preparation for His earthly conflict, offer in many respects a remarkable contrast to the forty days after the Resurrection, the preparation for His heavenly work. At first, like Moses or Elijah, He was 'led' or 'driven' into the wilderness: at last He was bound by no ties of space. 'Then', as Augustine says, 'He set forth in Himself the 'greatness of our struggle: now He shews in us 'the greatness of His consolation.' What were before the occasions for temptation are now the fruits of victory. Then He hungered and found no food: now He knew no bodily wants and yet ate before His disciples. Then he refused the kingdoms of the world which were offered to Him by Satan: now He bids His ministers proclaim His sovereignty over all the nations. Then He repelled the Tempter who bade Him cast Himself down from the pinnacle of the Temple: now He moves as one free from the restraints of earth. *In many parts and in many fashions* the power of the new life was manifested: the idea of the Resurrection was established.

Thus in due course the lesson was learnt and the appointed time of teaching came to an end. But at the last one desire, perhaps one misgiving, remained to the disciples. They had received, as we have seen, their spiritual commission. They had been instructed in the fulfilment of their office. They had been directed to the Scriptures as the certain exponents of the counsels of God. They had been strengthened by the promise of a Divine Guide without them, and of a Divine Power within them. But they were Jews, and they could not forget the hopes of their nation. While it was yet possible—and this is the one question which they are related to have put to the Risen Christ — they sought for light on this dark spot. *Therefore, we read, when they were come together*—probably in obedience to some command of Christ—*they asked Him, saying, Lord, dost Thou at this time restore the kingdom to Israel?* The words are not to be taken as the expression of an unworthy ambition, or of a false view of the Christian society. They are rather the utterance of a noble unselfishness. The disciples had known the gift of God; but it seemed to be incomplete if it was only for themselves. They had no doubt, indeed, as to the final issue, but they inquired as to the time. Delay was hard to understand; yet delay could be borne. The Lord's answer to their question exactly corresponds to His answer to the personal inquiry of St Peter by the Sea of Tiberias. He turned their thoughts from the contemplation of mysteries to the prospect of active duty. *He said unto them, It is not for you to know times or seasons which the Father hath set within His own authority.* The consummation for which you look—so it is implied—is, as you think, part of the Providential order, but it is not for man to learn the date or the manner of its fulfilment, the long years which must pass before all things are ready, or the concurrence of circumstances which shall prepare the end. *But* meanwhile you have a work to do, heavenly in its origin, and boundless in its application. *Ye shall receive power, when the Holy Ghost is come upon you: and ye shall be my witnesses both in Jerusalem and in all Judæa and Samaria, and unto the uttermost part of the earth. And when He had said these things*—we may here insert the words of the Gospel—*He lifted up His hands, and blessed them. And it came to pass, while He blessed them, He was parted from them; and as they were looking He was taken up and a cloud received Him out of their sight.*

X.

Luke xxiv. 50 f.

So the Resurrection was finally shewn in its permanence and in its glory. The Lord no longer vanished from sight as if He might shortly return again as he had done before. He withdrew in such a way as to suggest most impressively to those who were assembled with Him that He had entered on a new mode of connexion with His Church. As they gazed up into heaven He rose, as it appears, by the exertion of His own will, and not, as from the grave, by the power of the Father. There were no angels to carry Him from among men, as they carried the body of Moses: no chariot of fire to

x. bear Him in a whirlwind, as Elijah was borne. His hands were raised to bless; and in the fulness of benediction He passed beyond the sphere of man's sensible existence to the open Presence of God. The physical elevation was a speaking parable, an eloquent symbol, but not the Truth to which it pointed or the reality which it foreshadowed. The change which Christ revealed by the Ascension was not a change of place, but a change of state, not local but spiritual. But from the necessities of our human condition the spiritual change was represented sacramentally, so to speak, in an outward form.

This being so, we can see how the Ascension was at once an end and a beginning, the close of one dispensation and the dawn of another, the last event recorded in the Gospel and the first event recorded in the Acts. It limits and unites the Life of Christ and the Life of His Church; or rather, to express the same thought differently, the Life of Christ in His humiliation and the Life of Christ in His glory.

The Ascension of Christ is, in a word, His going to the Father—to His Father and our Father—the visible pledge and symbol of the exaltation of the earthly into the heavenly. It is emphatically a revelation of heavenly life, the open fulfilment of man's destiny made possible for all men. So it proved to be in the experience of the disciples. While the Lord was yet with them they found it a hard saying when He spoke of spiritual communion. But henceforward they were content to rest in His love and to labour after His bidding. They accepted gladly the discipline of patience and the law of order as the expression of the wisdom and of the love of God.

Such was the closing revelation of the Risen Lord; and as we ponder the history we come to see that it stands written for our learning. The last question of the disciples, the last words of the Master, enter deeply into our experience. The desire, the misgiving which found expression and were stilled on the eve of the Ascension, must often rise in our own hearts. The Kingdom of God seems to us to linger; to us who measure by days and by years. Our hope is deferred. Our expectations fail. At such moments of trial the Lord's commission at this revelation of the Ascension comes back with a new and living force. Through that we are enabled to learn that we have entered into fellowship with a world in which human standards of time have no place; that it is not for us to determine or to anticipate the method in which the end of the Divine counsels will be gained, but to use the gifts of a heavenly life and to bear without doubt and

x.

without weariness the message of a Gospel to the world.

In ordinary life nothing is treasured up with more sacred affection, nothing is more powerful to move us with silent and abiding persuasiveness, nothing is more able to unite together the seen and the unseen, than the last words, the last look of those who have passed away from us, the last revelation of the life which trembles, as it were, on the verge of its transfigurement. The last words of Christ were a promise and a charge. The last act of Christ was an act of blessing. The last revelation of Christ was the elevation of the temporal into the eternal, beyond sight and yet with the assurance of an unbroken fellowship. That promise, that charge, that blessing, that revelation, are for us, the unchanged and unchangeable bequest of the Risen Lord. His hands are stretched out still. His Spirit is still hovering about us. His work is still waiting to be accomplished. The Revelation of the Ascension brings Him Who has died and risen again within the reach of every loving child of man throughout all the ages and throughout all the earth. It makes that felt to be universal which was seen to be limited before. It shews that to be abiding which was hitherto manifested under transitory forms. Now,

John xx. 17.

when His triumph is completed, the believer may cling to the Lord with the embrace not of the hand but of the heart. Now He is given back for ever by the ministration of the Spirit.

Thus at length it was made plain how it was *expedient that He should go away.* By that return to the Father His Presence was made sovereign over all limits of time and place. We can claim it and enjoy it, as our fathers have done, as our children will do, if we bring before our souls the living image of His divine benediction; if we believe in the efficacy of His Life and Death and Resurrection; if we listen to the still voice which directs each one of us to the particular duty that he has to fulfil, which interprets to each one of us the witness that he has to give.

That which hath been is and ever will be. If the Presence of Christ seem in some sense to be taken from us in these later days, the apparent removal calls out a blessing never before given. Each moment, each semblance, of separation becomes for believers the revelation of Divine Majesty. The words written of the first disciples will be found true of every disciple in every age: *He led them out until they were over against Bethany*—out of the sacred precincts which enclosed all that they held most sacred,

x.

Luke xxiv. 50 ff.

x. past the scene of the Agony and the scene of the Weeping—*and He lifted up His hands and blessed them. And it came to pass while He blessed them, He parted from them, and was carried up into heaven. And they worshipped Him, and returned to Jerusalem*—returned having lost the Lord from their sight that they might have Him for ever—*with great joy; and were continually in the Temple, blessing God.*

XI.

THE REVELATION FROM HEAVEN AND ON EARTH.

Ἐν δὲ τῷ πορεύεσθαι ἐγένετο αὐτὸν ἐγγίζειν τῇ Δαμασκῷ, ἐξέφνης τε αὐτὸν περιήστραψεν φῶς ἐκ τοῦ οὐρανοῦ, καὶ πεσὼν ἐπὶ τὴν γῆν ἤκουσεν φωνὴν λέγουσαν αὐτῷ Σαούλ Σαούλ, τί με διώκεις; εἶπεν δέ Τίς εἶ, κύριε; ὁ δέ Ἐγώ εἰμι Ἰησοῦς ὃν σὺ διώκεις· ἀλλὰ ἀνάστηθι καὶ εἴσελθε εἰς τὴν πόλιν, καὶ λαληθήσεταί σοι ὅτι σε δεῖ ποιεῖν. οἱ δὲ ἄνδρες οἱ συνοδεύοντες αὐτῷ ἱστήκεισαν ἐνεοί, ἀκούοντες μὲν τῆς φωνῆς μηδένα δὲ θεωροῦντες. ἠγέρθη δὲ Σαῦλος ἀπὸ τῆς γῆς, ἀνεῳγμένων δὲ τῶν ὀφθαλμῶν αὐτοῦ οὐδὲν ἔβλεπεν· χειραγωγοῦντες δὲ αὐτὸν εἰσήγαγον εἰς Δαμασκόν. καὶ ἦν ἡμέρας τρεῖς μὴ βλέπων, καὶ οὐκ ἔφαγεν οὐδὲ ἔπιεν.

Ἐγένετο δέ μοι πορευομένῳ καὶ ἐγγίζοντι τῇ Δαμασκῷ περὶ μεσημβρίαν ἐξαίφνης ἐκ τοῦ οὐρανοῦ περιαστράψαι φῶς ἱκανὸν περὶ ἐμέ, ἔπεσά τε εἰς τὸ ἔδαφος καὶ ἤκουσα φωνῆς λεγούσης μοι Σαούλ Σαούλ, τί με διώκεις; ἐγὼ δὲ ἀπεκρίθην Τίς εἶ, κύριε; εἶπέν τε πρὸς ἐμέ Ἐγώ εἰμι Ἰησοῦς ὁ Ναζωραῖος ὃν σὺ διώκεις. οἱ δὲ σὺν ἐμοὶ ὄντες τὸ μὲν φῶς ἐθεάσαντο τὴν δὲ φωνὴν οὐκ ἤκουσαν τοῦ λαλοῦντός μοι. εἶπον δέ Τί ποιήσω, κύριε; ὁ δὲ κύριος εἶπεν πρός με Ἀναστὰς πορεύου εἰς Δαμασκόν, κἀκεῖ σοι λαληθήσεται περὶ πάντων ὧν τέτακταί σοι ποιῆσαι. ὡς δὲ οὐκ ἐνέβλεπον ἀπὸ τῆς δόξης τοῦ φωτὸς ἐκείνου, χειραγωγούμενος ὑπὸ τῶν συνόντων μοι ἦλθον εἰς Δαμασκόν.

And as he journeyed, it came to pass that he drew nigh unto Damascus: and suddenly there shone round about him a light out of heaven: and he fell upon the earth, and heard a voice saying unto him, Saul, Saul, why persecutest thou me? And he said, Who art thou, Lord? And he said, I am Jesus whom thou persecutest: but rise, and enter into the city, and it shall be told thee what thou must do. And the men that journeyed with him stood speechless, hearing the voice, but beholding no man. And Saul arose from the earth; and when his eyes were opened, he saw nothing; and they led him by the hand, and brought him into Damascus. And he was three days without sight, and did neither eat nor drink.

ACTS ix. 3—9.

And it came to pass, that, as I made my journey, and drew nigh unto Damascus, about noon, suddenly there shone from heaven a great light round about me. And I fell unto the ground, and heard a voice saying unto me, Saul, Saul, why persecutest thou me? And I answered, Who art thou, Lord? And he said unto me, I am Jesus of ·Nazareth, whom thou persecutest. And they that were with me beheld indeed the light, but they heard not the voice of him that spake to me. And I said, What shall I do, Lord? And the Lord said unto me, Arise, and go into Damascus; and there it shall be told thee of all things which are appointed for thee to do. And when I could not see for the glory of that light, being led by the hand of them that were with me, I came into Damascus.

ACTS xxii. 6—11.

Ἐν οἷc πορευόμενοc εἰc τὴν Δαμαcκὸν μετ' ἐξουcίαc καὶ ἐπιτροπῆc τῆc τῶν ἀρχιερέων ἡμέραc μέcηc κατὰ τὴν ὁδὸν εἶδον, Βαcιλεῦ, οὐρανόθεν ὑπὲρ τὴν λαμπρότητα τοῦ ἡλίου περιλάμψαν με φῶc καὶ τοὺc cὺν ἐμοὶ πορευομένουc· πάντων τε καταπεcόντων ἡμῶν εἰc τὴν γῆν ἤκουcα φωνὴν λέγουcαν πρόc με τῇ Ἑβραΐδι διαλέκτῳ Σαούλ Σαούλ, τί με διώκειc; cκληρόν cοι πρὸc κέντρα λακτίζειν. ἐγὼ δὲ εἶπα Τίc εἶ, κύριε; ὁ δὲ κύριοc εἶπεν Ἐγώ εἰμι Ἰηcοῦc ὃν cὺ διώκειc. ἀλλὰ ἀνάcτηθι καὶ cτῆθι ἐπὶ τοὺc πόδαc cου· εἰc τοῦτο γὰρ ὤφθην cοι, προχειρίcαcθαί cε ὑπηρέτην καὶ μάρτυρα ὧν τε εἶδέc με ὧν τε ὀφθήcομαί cοι, ἐξαιρούμενόc cε ἐκ τοῦ λαοῦ καὶ ἐκ τῶν ἐθνῶν, εἰc οὓc ἐγὼ ἀποcτέλλω cε ἀνοῖξαι ὀφθαλμοὺc αὐτῶν, τοῦ ἐπιcτρέψαι ἀπὸ cκότουc εἰc φῶc καὶ τῆc ἐξουcίαc τοῦ Σατανᾶ ἐπὶ τὸν θεόν, τοῦ λαβεῖν αὐτοὺc ἄφεcιν ἁμαρτιῶν καὶ κλῆρον ἐν τοῖc ἡγιαcμένοιc πίcτει τῇ εἰc ἐμέ.

Whereupon as I journeyed to Damascus with the authority and commission of the chief priests, at midday, O king, I saw on the way a light from heaven, above the brightness of the sun, shining round about me and them that journeyed with me. And when we were all fallen to the earth, I heard a voice saying unto me in the Hebrew language, Saul, Saul, why persecutest thou me? it is hard for thee to kick against the goad. And I said, Who art thou, Lord? And the Lord said, I am Jesus whom thou persecutest. But arise, and stand upon thy feet: for to this end have I appeared unto thee, to appoint thee a minister and a witness both of the things wherein thou hast seen me, and of the things wherein I will appear unto thee; delivering thee from the people, and from the Gentiles, unto whom I send thee, to open their eyes, that they may turn from darkness to light, and from the power of Satan unto God, that they may receive remission of sins and an inheritance among them that are sanctified by faith in me.

ACTS xxvi. 12—18.

Χριστῷ συνεσταύρωμαι· ζῶ δὲ οὐκέτι ἐγώ, ζῇ δὲ ἐν ἐμοὶ Χριστός.

I have been crucified with Christ; yet I live; and yet no longer I, but Christ liveth in me.

GAL. ii. 20.

THE REVELATION FROM HEAVEN AND ON EARTH.

WE have seen that the recorded manifesta- XI.
tions of the Risen Christ were fitted to furnish the first disciples and the Church in all ages with a sure foundation for the belief in His true personal Resurrection, and of His abiding connexion with His people. In typical cases He quickened and confirmed individual faith (I. II.) and social faith (III. IV.); and in doing this He made clear the inadequacy of all outward tests in themselves to establish the truth to which outward experience was the approach (V). Starting from the belief in the fact of His Resurrection, which was thus created and defined, He afterwards laid open in successive scenes the reality of His Presence with believers through the manifold work of life (VI. VII. VIII.). At last He marked by signal and expressive acts the close of His former earthly relationship with those whom He had chosen as being the condition of a new relation-

192 Cessation of the appearances

XI. ship fulfilled through the Spirit (IX. X.). Each narrative conveys a distinct lesson fitting in harmoniously with all the others, and in its proper measure throwing light upon the unseen world in which and to which we are moving.

At this point then there is a decisive break in the history. No fresh events of a like kind follow. Faith has been quickened by a revelation complete and adequate, and it was effective in operation. This sudden change in the experience of the Church is equally significant negatively and positively. The abrupt cessation of the appearances of Christ is intelligible if they were granted for the specific end of producing the faith which they did produce: it is not intelligible if they were the creation of enthusiasm.

Acts vii. 54 ff.

The vision of St Stephen is no exception to the statement which has been made. That is presented as an exceptional encouragement vouchsafed to the first martyr, wholly isolated and yet in its form of the deepest significance. St Paul, it is likely, heard St Stephen's words, but in his enumeration of the Lord's appearances he gives no place to this. A similar remark applies to the

Acts ix. 10 ff.

communication to Ananias. Of him it is recorded expressly, *the Lord said unto him in a vision;* and the note is the more striking as it follows closely on the narrative of the call of St Paul. Besides

till the unique appearance to St Paul.

these visions there were many other manifestations of the powers of the spiritual world; but for a long space, probably for six or eight years, the Lord, as far as we know, did not reveal Himself. Then finally 'He was seen last of all' by St Paul.

Here again it is of the utmost importance historically to observe that the appearance was unique. There was in the apostolic Church the keenest expectation of the immediate visible Return of the Lord. Some even taught *that the day of the Lord is now present.* But there is not the least trace that any one professed to have seen Him. Every circumstance, it may be fairly said, was now favourable to creations of enthusiasm, but none were alleged. The experience of St Paul is no less instructive. He had visions on other occasions. Once he says that he *saw the Lord speaking to him*, but this was when he had *fallen into a trance.* He *received his gospel through the revelation of Jesus Christ.* On another occasion it is recorded in the Acts that *the Lord spake to him by night in a vision;* and yet again that *the Lord by night stood by him, and said, Be of good courage.* But these exhibitions of the Lord's power are separated decisively and yet without any conscious purpose, as it seems, from the appearance on the road to Damascus. That was on the same line as the appearances

XI.
Acts v. 19;
viii. 26;
xii. 7 (17);
viii. 39;
x. 3 ff.;
xxviii. 23;
x. 11 ff.;
1 Cor. xv. 8.

2 Thess. ii. 2.

Acts xxii. 18.
Gal. i. 11 f.

Acts xviii. 9.
Acts xxiii. 11.

W.   13

during the forty days, objective and personal, on the one side coming fully within the range of our present human life, and on the other transcending it.

For this appearance, like those which have been already considered, was a revelation. It brought a new view of the Life and Presence of Christ. It was a revelation through sense and yet in no way measured by sense. That in which St Paul recognised the Lord was for those who journeyed with him simply a light. The voice for them was a mere sound not articulate in words. Out of the heavenly glory Christ made Himself known to the future Apostle as *Jesus Whom thou persecutest*: from heaven He spoke of Himself as still on earth.

It is in the simultaneous affirmation of these two contrasted and complementary truths that the revelation lies. St Paul's characteristic teaching is a proof of the power with which both were borne in upon his soul. If before he knew a Christ after the flesh he now knew Him so no more. The idea of the glorified Christ fills all his thoughts. And again the conception of believers as members of Christ, and of the Church as His Body, moulds his whole theory of the Christian life. He first, and the fact is one of those unaccentuated and yet most significant points in the progress of the faith which are apt to be overlooked, *proclaimed Jesus in the Synagogues that He is the Son of God*. The mode in which 'Jesus'—still truly man—was made known to him carried with it the conviction, complete at once, that He was also in nature truly Divine.

XI.

Acts ix. 20.

In each respect this last Revelation of the Risen Lord crowned the Revelations which had been given before. Those were all suited in various ways to shew how the Lord who had *gone in and out* among the disciples had entered upon a divine life: this was suited to make Him known in His divine being. By the address to St Thomas and by the manifestation at the Sea of Tiberias He had in deed and symbol disclosed His abiding Presence with His people: here He laid open the most mysterious fact of human existence, that believers are in Him and He in them. The appearance to St Paul was in a word a revelation of a continuous life of the Risen Christ on earth in virtue of His being the Son of God.

The natural dependence of the one truth upon the other is obvious. The apprehension of the divine nature of Christ enables us to understand in some measure how He still enters into human life and fulfils His work in and through men, how He is Sovereign and yet persecuted. And from the human point of sight sufferings and labours are shewn to be fruitful because they are brought into a living connexion with Christ.

Perhaps it is in this latter respect that the power of the Revelation is most fully shewn. The words *Why persecutest thou Me?* bear in them sufficient consolation for those who endure for the Truth, 'not they but Christ.' And the lesson was made plain to St Paul when, as the issue of his conversion, it was shewn him *how many things he must suffer* for the name of Christ. Such sufferings, it was now evidently seen, were sufferings not only for Christ but of Christ, and therefore charged with a heavenly virtue.

How completely this new thought of the character of faithful suffering entered into St Paul's estimate of the power of life is seen from his account of his own feelings. *I rejoice in my sufferings for your sake, and fill up that which is lacking of the afflictions of Christ in my flesh for His Body's sake, which is the Church.* Christ worked through him, yet so that he now was able under the conditions of earth to suffer in Christ's stead. What Christ could no longer do the disciple did by the inspiration of His Life, not indeed as if his acts were in themselves meritorious or (still less) had any power of vicarious satisfaction, but as discharging an office which by divine appointment was rich in beneficent results for the building up of the Christian Society.

Thus the revelation of the Risen Christ to St Paul may be described as a revelation of glory and of weakness, of glory and weakness reconciled; and in view of the actual condition of the Church it is not difficult to perceive the part which it fulfils in the interpretation of the Gospel. Without it the long times of silence and apparent loneliness, of dull distress and oppression, might seem to be inconsistent with the present sovereignty of Christ. As it is, these are shewn to be a discipline with a divine purpose. If *it behoved the Christ to suffer and to enter into His glory*, the same law applies to the Church in which His earthly Life, so to speak, is continued 'in the flesh.'

Luke xxiv. 26.

It is unnecessary to dwell on the practical consequences of this view of the position and work of the Church. One only may be noticed. It has been boldly urged against the Christian Faith that the object of worship which it proposes is removed far from all need of service; and that consequently believers are deprived of one of the noblest motives of labour. This Revelation of the Lord from glory wholly disposes of the objection. Our Lord, shewn to the eye of faith in His Majesty, is persecuted still. He needs,—

the mystery is involved in the Incarnation,—the ministry of love; and He blesses the patience of suffering.

There is yet another truth established by the Revelation to St Paul. It is the sensible confirmation of the reality of the personal fellowship of the Risen Lord and the believer. Just as the Conversion of St Paul is the type of the common martyrdom of life, so his Call is the type of the common miracle of life. By this, in a signal example, it was shewn openly that the Lord, though departed to the Father, still holds intercourse with His disciples. As it was during His earthly Life, as it was during the period of transition from suffering to glory, so it is now: He watches over them and is with them, though the form of His Presence is changed. That which was before local and temporal is now spiritual and eternal, while still it is capable of being manifested under the conditions of sense.

Thus the cycle of revelations is completed. The Risen Lord has so shewn Himself as to create in individual disciples and in the Christian Society the conviction of His new Life, in which all that belonged to the essence of his humanity was preserved and transfigured. He has so shewn Himself as to establish the belief in His providential

miracle of life. 199

guidance of the fortunes of the Church and of His Presence with all who work and wait in His service. He has at last from the throne of His spiritual Kingdom so shewn Himself as to make evident the divine reality which underlies the voices and visions of heaven, the divine purpose which is slowly wrought out on the stage of earth. The thought of that Life, of that Providence, of that Presence, of that Communion, of that Mystery of pain, has passed into the world and become part of the heritage of manhood. *The old things are passed away: behold, they are become new.*

XI.

2 Cor. v. 17.

December, 1881.

A CATALOGUE of THEOLOGICAL BOOKS,
Published by
MACMILLAN AND CO.
Bedford Street, Strand, London, W.C.

Abbott (Rev. E. A.)—Works by the Rev. E. A. ABBOTT, D.D., Head Master of the City of London School:

BIBLE LESSONS. Second Edition. Crown 8vo. 4s. 6d.

"*Wise, suggestive, and really profound initiation into religious thought.*"—Guardian. *The Bishop of St. David's, in his speech at the Education Conference at Abergwilly, says he thinks "nobody could read them without being the better for them himself, and being also able to see how this difficult duty of imparting a sound religious education may be effected."*

THE GOOD VOICES: A Child's Guide to the Bible. With upwards of 50 Illustrations. Crown 8vo, cloth gilt. 5s.

"*It would not be easy to combine simplicity with fulness and depth of meaning more successfully than Mr. Abbott has done.*"—Spectator. *The* Times *says*—"*Mr. Abbott writes with clearness, simplicity, and the deepest religious feeling.*"

CAMBRIDGE SERMONS PREACHED BEFORE THE UNIVERSITY. Second Edition. 8vo. 6s.

OXFORD SERMONS PREACHED BEFORE THE UNIVERSITY. 8vo. 7s. 6d.

THROUGH NATURE TO CHRIST; or, The Ascent of Worship through Illusion to the Truth. 8vo. 12s. 6d.

"*The beauty of its style, its tender feeling, and its perfect sympathy, the originality and suggestiveness of many of its thoughts, would of themselves go far to recommend it. But far besides these, it has a certain value in its bold, comprehensive, trenchant method of apology, and in the adroitness with which it turns the flank of the many modern fallacies that caricature in order to condemn Christianity.*"—Church Quarterly Review.

Ainger (Rev. Alfred).—SERMONS PREACHED IN THE TEMPLE CHURCH. By the Rev. ALFRED AINGER, M.A. of Trinity Hall, Cambridge, Reader at the Temple Church. Extra fcap. 8vo. 6s.

"*It is,*" *the* British Quarterly *says,* "*the fresh unconventional talk of a*

THEOLOGICAL BOOKS.

clear independent thinker, addressed to a congregation of thinkers.... Thoughtful men will be greatly charmed by this little volume."

Arnold.—Works by MATTHEW ARNOLD:

A BIBLE READING FOR SCHOOLS. THE GREAT PROPHECY OF ISRAEL'S RESTORATION (Isaiah, Chapters 40—66). Arranged and Edited for Young Learners. By MATTHEW ARNOLD, D.C.L. Third Edition. 18mo. 1s.

The Times says—"Whatever may be the fate of this little book in Government Schools, there can be no doubt that it will be found excellently calculated to further instruction in Biblical literature in any school into which it may be introduced.

ISAIAH XL.—LXVI., with the Shorter Prophecies allied to it. Arranged and Edited with Notes. Crown 8vo. 5s.

Bather.—ON SOME MINISTERIAL DUTIES; CATECHISING, PREACHING, &c. Charges by the late Archdeacon BATHER. Edited, with Preface, by Dr. C. J. VAUGHAN. Extra fcap. 8vo. 4s. 6d.

Bernard.—THE PROGRESS OF DOCTRINE IN THE NEW TESTAMENT. By THOMAS D. BERNARD, M.A., Rector of Walcot and Canon of Wells. Third and Cheaper Edition. Crown 8vo. 5s. (Bampton Lectures for 1864.)

Binney.—A SECOND SERIES OF SERMONS. By THOMAS BINNEY, D.D. Edited with Biographical and Critical Sketch, by the Rev. HENRY ALLON, D.D. With Portrait of Dr. Binney engraved by JEENS. 8vo. 12s.

Birks.—Works by T. R. BIRKS, M.A., Professor of Moral Philosophy, Cambridge:

THE DIFFICULTIES OF BELIEF in connection with the Creation and the Fall, Redemption and Judgment. Second Edition, enlarged. Crown 8vo. 5s.

AN ESSAY ON THE RIGHT ESTIMATION OF MS. EVIDENCE IN THE TEXT OF THE NEW TESTAMENT. Crown 8vo. 3s. 6d.

COMMENTARY ON THE BOOK OF ISAIAH, Critical, Historical, and Prophetical; including a Revised English Translation. With Introduction and Appendices on the Nature of Scripture Prophecy, the Life and Times of Isaiah, the Genuineness of the Later Prophecies, the Structure and History of the whole Book, the Assyrian History in Isaiah's Days, and various Difficult Passages. Second Edition, revised. 8vo. 12s. 6d.

THEOLOGICAL BOOKS. 3

BIRKS (Prof.)—*continued.*
SUPERNATURAL REVELATION; or, First Principles of Moral Theology. 8vo. 8*s.*

Blackie.—LAY SERMONS. By JOHN STUART BLACKIE, Professor of Greek in the University of Edinburgh. Crown 8vo. 6*s.*

The subjects of these "Sermons," so called as the author tells us "because, though some of them were delivered in the form of popular lectures, they have all a direct practical drift, and are intended either to apply Christian ethics or to expound Christian doctrine in reference to matters of special interest at the present time."—are as follows : (1) *The Creation of the World,* (2) *The Jewish Sabbath and the Christian Lord's Day,* (3) *Faith,* (4) *The Utilisation of Evil,* (5) *Landlords and Land-laws,* (6) *The Politics of Christianity,* (7) *The Dignity of Labour,* (8) *The Scottish Covenanters,* (9) *On Symbolism, Ceremonialism, Formalism, and the New Creature; with an* Appendix *on The Metaphysics of Genesis I.*

Bradby.—SERMONS PREACHED AT HAILEYBURY. By E. H. BRADBY, M.A., Master. 8vo. 10*s.* 6*d.*

Brooks.—THE CANDLE OF THE LORD, AND OTHER SERMONS. By the Rev. PHILLIPS BROOKS, Rector of Trinity Church, Boston. Crown 8vo. 6*s.*

Mr. Brooks' reputation as a preacher stands very high among his own countrymen, and several of his previous volumes which have found their way across the Atlantic, such as Lectures on Preaching, &c., *have attracted attention here. It may be hoped, therefore, that this new volume will be welcome to English readers. The first sermon, which gives its title to the volume, was delivered in Westminster Abbey, and was greatly admired by Dean Stanley who was a personal friend of the preacher.*

Brunton.—THE BIBLE AND SCIENCE. By T. Lauder Brunton, M.D., D.Sc., F.R.S., etc. With Illustrations. Crown 8vo. 10*s.* 6*d.*

The objects of the present work are to give a brief and popular sketch of the data on which the doctrine of Evolution is founded, and to shew that instead of being atheistic it is the very reverse, and is no more opposed to the Biblical account of the Creation than those geological doctrines regarding the structure and formation of the earth's crust which were once regarded as heretical and dangerous, but are now to be found in every class-book, and are taught in every school. The plan adopted has been to give a brief account, first, of the living things both animal and vegetable which now exist on this earth, and of their relation to one another; and, secondly, of the forms of life which existed in the early ages of the world's history, and their relationships to one another, as well as to those of the present day. After this follows a discussion of the question, how these various forms of life, past and present, came into existence, whether by sudden creation or gradual evolution.

Butcher.—THE ECCLESIASTICAL CALENDAR; its Theory and Construction. By SAMUEL BUTCHER, D.D., late Bishop of Meath. 4to. 14s.

Butler (Rev. G.)—Works by the Rev. GEORGE BUTLER, M.A., Principal of Liverpool College:

FAMILY PRAYERS. Crown 8vo. 5s.

SERMONS PREACHED in CHELTENHAM COLLEGE CHAPEL. Crown 8vo. 7s. 6d.

Butler (Rev. H. M.)—SERMONS PREACHED in the CHAPEL OF HARROW SCHOOL. By H. MONTAGU BUTLER, Head Master. Crown 8vo. 7s. 6d.

"*These sermons are adapted for every household. There is nothing more striking than the excellent good sense with which they are imbued.*" —Spectator.

A SECOND SERIES. Crown 8vo. 7s. 6d.

"*Excellent specimens of what sermons should be—plain, direct, practical, pervaded by the true spirit of the Gospel, and holding up lofty aims before the minds of the young.*"—Athenæum.

Butler (Rev. W. Archer).—Works by the Rev. WILLIAM ARCHER BUTLER, M.A., late Professor of Moral Philosophy in the University of Dublin:

SERMONS, DOCTRINAL AND PRACTICAL. Edited, with a Memoir of the Author's Life, by THOMAS WOODWARD, Dean of Down. With Portrait. Ninth Edition. 8vo. 8s.

A SECOND SERIES OF SERMONS. Edited by J. A. JEREMIE, D.D., Dean of Lincoln. Seventh Edition. 8vo. 7s.

LETTERS ON ROMANISM, in reply to Dr. Newman's 'Essay on Development.' Edited by the Dean of Down. Second Edition, revised by Archdeacon HARDWICK. 8vo. 10s. 6d.

These Letters contain an exhaustive criticism of Dr. Newman's famous 'Essay on the Development of Christian Doctrine.' "A work which ought to be in the Library of every student of Divinity."—BP. ST. DAVID'S.

Calderwood.—Works by HENRY CALDERWOOD, LL.D., Professor of Moral Philosophy in the University of Edinburgh:

THEOLOGICAL BOOKS. 5

CALDERWOOD (Dr.)—*continued.*

THE PARABLES OF OUR LORD, interpreted in view of their relations to each other. Crown 8vo. 6s.

"*They are written in a simple intelligible manner, and may be read with satisfaction.*"—Westminster Review.

THE RELATIONS OF SCIENCE AND RELIGION. Being the Morse Lecture, 1880, connected with Union Theological Seminary, New York. Crown 8vo. 5s.

Cambridge Lent Sermons, 1864.—Sermons preached during Lent, 1864, in Great St. Mary's Church, Cambridge. By the Right Rev. the Lord Bishop of Oxford, Rev. H. P. Liddon, Rev. T. L. Claughton, Rev. J. R. Woodford, Rev. Dr. Goulburn, Very Rev. Dean Hook, Rev. W. J. Butler, and others. Crown 8vo. 7s. 6d.

Campbell.—Works by JOHN M'LEOD CAMPBELL:

THE NATURE OF THE ATONEMENT AND ITS RELATION TO REMISSION OF SINS AND ETERNAL LIFE. Fourth and Cheaper Edition. Crown 8vo. 6s.

"*Among the first theological treatises of this generation.*"—Guardian. "*One of the most remarkable theological books ever written.*"—Times.

CHRIST THE BREAD OF LIFE. An Attempt to give a profitable direction to the present occupation of Thought with Romanism. Second Edition, greatly enlarged. Crown 8vo. 4s. 6d.

"*Deserves the most attentive study by all who interest themselves in the predominant religious controversy of the day.*"—Spectator.

REMINISCENCES AND REFLECTIONS, referring to his Early Ministry in the Parish of Row, 1825—31. Edited with an Introductory Narrative by his Son, DONALD CAMPBELL, M.A., Chaplain of King's College, London. Crown 8vo. 7s. 6d.

"*We recommend this book cordially to all who are interested in the great cause of religious reformation.*"—Times. "*There is a thoroughness and depth, as well as a practical earnestness, in his grasp of each truth on which he dilates, which make his reflections very valuable.*"— Literary Churchman.

THOUGHTS ON REVELATION, with Special Reference to the Present Time. Second Edition. Crown 8vo. 5s.

RESPONSIBILITY FOR THE GIFT OF ETERNAL LIFE. Compiled by permission of the late J. M'LEOD CAMPBELL, D.D., from Sermons preached chiefly at Row in 1829—31. Crown 8vo. 5s.

6 THEOLOGICAL BOOKS.

Campbell (Lewis).—SOME ASPECTS OF THE CHRISTIAN IDEAL. Sermons by the Rev. L. CAMPBELL, M.A., LL.D., Professor of Greek in the University of Glasgow. Crown 8vo. 6s.

Canterbury.—Works by ARCHIBALD CAMPBELL, Archbishop of Canterbury :

THE CHURCH OF THE FUTURE. Its Catholicity; its Conflict with the Atheist ; its Conflict with the Deist ; its Conflict with the Rationalist ; its Dogmatic Teaching ; Practical Councils for its Work; its Cathedrals. Constituting the Charge delivered at his Third Quadrennial Visitation, A.D. 1880. Second Edition. Crown 8vo. 3s. 6d.

THE PRESENT POSITION OF THE CHURCH OF ENGLAND. Seven Addresses delivered to the Clergy and Churchwardens of his Diocese, as his Charge, at his Primary Visitation, 1872. Third Edition. 8vo. 3s. 6d.

SOME THOUGHTS ON THE DUTIES OF THE ESTABLISHED CHURCH OF ENGLAND AS A NATIONAL CHURCH. Seven Addresses delivered at his Second Visitation. 8vo. 4s. 6d.

Cellarius.—A NEW ANALOGY BETWEEN REVEALED RELIGION AND THE COURSE AND CONSTITUTION OF NATURE. By CELLARIUS. Crown 8vo. 6s.

The argument from Analogy, as first applied by Butler, being, so far as regards its method, of eternal value and significance, there seems no reason why it may not once more be employed to combat the present state of mental incredulity and indifference, due care being taken to adapt the course and details of the argument to the changes which lapse of time and alterations in the way of thinking have produced in the attitude of those who cannot bring themselves to regard the Christian religion as being the direct work of God. The present writer here addresses to his fellow Christians, more especially laymen, those reasons which have from time to time, appeared to himself to afford a reasonably strong presumption that Nature and Revelation have proceeded from the same Author, and that, therefore, the materials of a credible and rational religion are placed at the disposal of mankind.

Cheyne.—Works by T. K. CHEYNE, M.A., Fellow of Balliol College, Oxford:

THE BOOK OF ISAIAH CHRONOLOGICALLY ARRANGED. An Amended Version, with Historical and Critical Introductions and Explanatory Notes. Crown 8vo. 7s. 6d.

NOTES AND CRITICISMS on the HEBREW TEXT OF ISAIAH. Crown 8vo. 2s. 6d.

THEOLOGICAL BOOKS. 7

Choice Notes on the Four Gospels, drawn from Old and New Sources. Crown 8vo. 4s. 6d. each Vol. (St. Matthew and St. Mark in one Vol. price 9s.)

Church.—Works by the Very Rev. R. W. CHURCH, M.A., D.C.L., Dean of St. Paul's:

ON SOME INFLUENCES OF CHRISTIANITY UPON NATIONAL CHARACTER. Three Lectures delivered in St. Paul's Cathedral, Feb. 1873. Crown 8vo. 4s. 6d.

"*Few books that we have met with have given us keener pleasure than this....... It would be a real pleasure to quote extensively, so wise and so true, so tender and so discriminating are Dean Church's judgments, but the limits of our space are inexorable. We hope the book will be bought.*"—Literary Churchman.

THE SACRED POETRY OF EARLY RELIGIONS. Two Lectures in St. Paul's Cathedral. 18mo. 1s. I. The Vedas. II. The Psalms.

ST. ANSELM. Second Edition. Crown 8vo. 6s.

"*It is a sketch by the hand of a master, with every line marked by taste, learning, and real apprehension of the subject.*"—Pall Mall Gazette.

HUMAN LIFE AND ITS CONDITIONS. Sermons preached before the University of Oxford, 1876—78, with Three Ordination Sermons. Crown 8vo. 6s.

THE GIFTS OF CIVILIZATION, and other Sermons and Lectures delivered at Oxford and in St. Paul's Cathedral. New Edition. Crown 8vo. 7s. 6d.

Clergyman's Self-Examination concerning the APOSTLES' CREED. Extra fcap. 8vo. 1s. 6d.

Colenso.—THE COMMUNION SERVICE FROM THE BOOK OF COMMON PRAYER; with Select Readings from the Writings of the Rev. F. D. MAURICE, M.A. Edited by the Right Rev. J. W. COLENSO, D.D., Lord Bishop of Natal. New Edition. 16mo. 2s. 6d.

Collects of the Church of England. With a beautifully Coloured Floral Design to each Collect, and Illuminated Cover. Crown 8vo. 12s. Also kept in various styles of morocco.

Congreve.—HIGH HOPES, AND PLEADINGS FOR A REASONABLE FAITH, NOBLER THOUGHTS, LARGER CHARITY. Sermons preached in the Parish Church of Tooting Graveney, Surrey. By J. CONGREVE, M.A., Rector. Cheaper Issue. Crown 8vo. 5s.

THEOLOGICAL BOOKS.

Cooke.—RELIGION AND CHEMISTRY: A Re-statement of an Old Argument. By J. P. COOKE, Erving Professor of Chemistry and Mineralogy in Harvard University. Crown 8vo. 7s. 6d.

Cotton.—Works by the late GEORGE EDWARD LYNCH COTTON, D.D., Bishop of Calcutta:

SERMONS PREACHED TO ENGLISH CONGREGATIONS IN INDIA. Crown 8vo. 7s. 6d.

EXPOSITORY SERMONS ON THE EPISTLES FOR THE SUNDAYS OF THE CHRISTIAN YEAR. Two Vols. Crown 8vo. 15s.

Cunningham.—Works by the Rev. WILLIAM CUNNINGHAM, M.A.:

CHRISTIAN CIVILISATION. With special reference to India. Fcap. 8vo. 5s.

THE CHURCHES OF ASIA. A Methodical Sketch of the Second Century. Crown 8vo. 6s.

"*Not merely is such a treatise interesting to the believer; its interest extends to all.*"—Morning Post. "*We think it on the whole a painstaking and accurate delineation of the development of the ecclesiastical constitution of the Church.*"—London Quarterly.

Curteis.—DISSENT in its RELATION to the CHURCH OF ENGLAND. Eight Lectures preached before the University of Oxford, in the year 1871, on the foundation of the late Rev. John Bampton, M.A., Canon of Salisbury. By GEORGE HERBERT CURTEIS, M.A., late Fellow and Sub-Rector of Exeter College; Principal of the Lichfield Theological College, and Prebendary of Lichfield Cathedral; Rector of Turweston, Bucks. New Edition. Crown 8vo. 7s. 6d.

"*Mr. Curteis has done good service by maintaining in an eloquent, temperate, and practical manner, that discussion among Christians is really an evil, and that an intelligent basis can be found for at least a proximate union.*"—Saturday Review. "*A well-timed, learned, and thoughtful book.*"

Davies.—Works by the Rev. J. LLEWELYN DAVIES, M.A., Rector of Christ Church, St. Marylebone, etc.:

THE GOSPEL AND MODERN LIFE; with a Preface on a Recent Phase of Deism. Second Edition. To which is

THEOLOGICAL BOOKS. 9

DAVIES (Rev. J. Ll.)—*continued.*
added, Morality according to the Sacrament of the Lord's Supper; or, Three Discourses on the Names, Eucharist, Sacrifice, and Communion. Extra fcap. 8vo. 6s.

WARNINGS AGAINST SUPERSTITION. IN FOUR SERMONS FOR THE DAY. Extra fcap. 8vo. 2s. 6d.

"*We have seldom read a wiser little book. The Sermons are short, terse, and full of true spiritual wisdom, expressed with a lucidity and a moderation that must give them weight even with those who agree least with their author....... Of the volume as a whole it is hardly possible to speak with too cordial an appreciation.*"—Spectator.

THE CHRISTIAN CALLING. Sermons. Extra fcap. 8vo. 6s.

Donaldson.—THE APOSTOLICAL FATHERS: a Critical Account of their Genuine Writings and of their Doctrines. By JAMES DONALDSON, LL.D. Crown 8vo. 7s. 6d.

Eadie.—Works by JOHN EADIE, D.D., LL.D., Professor of Biblical Literature and Exegesis, United Presbyterian Church:

THE ENGLISH BIBLE. An External and Critical History of the various English Translations of Scripture, with Remarks on the Need of Revising the English New Testament. Two vols. 8vo. 28s.

"*Accurate, scholarly, full of completest sympathy with the translators and their work, and marvellously interesting.*"—Literary Churchman.
"*The work is a very valuable one. It is the result of vast labour, sound scholarship, and large erudition.*"—British Quarterly Review.

ST. PAUL'S EPISTLES TO THE THESSALONIANS. A Commentary on the Greek Text. Edited by the Rev. W. YOUNG, M.A., with a Preface by the Rev. Professor CAIRNS, D.D. 8vo. 12s.

Ecce Homo. A SURVEY OF THE LIFE AND WORK OF JESUS CHRIST. Fourteenth Edition. Crown 8vo. 6s.

"*A very original and remarkable book, full of striking thought and delicate perception; a book which has realised with wonderful vigour and freshness the historical magnitude of Christ's work, and which here and there gives us readings of the finest kind of the probable motive of His individual words and actions.*"—Spectator. "*The best and most established believer will find it adding some fresh buttresses to his faith.*"—Literary

THEOLOGICAL BOOKS.

Churchman. "*If we have not misunderstood him, we have before us a writer who has a right to claim deference from those who think deepest and know most.*"—Guardian.

Ecclesiastes. A TREATISE ON THE AUTHORSHIP OF ECCLESIASTES. To which is added a Dissertation on that which was spoken through Jeremiah the Prophet, as quoted in Matthew XXVII. 9, 10. Crown 8vo. 14s.

Faber.—SERMONS AT A NEW SCHOOL. By the Rev. ARTHUR FABER, M.A., Head Master of Malvern College. Crown 8vo. 6s.

Farrar.—Works by the Rev. F. W. FARRAR, D.D., F.R.S., Canon of Westminster, late Head Master of Marlborough College:

THE FALL OF MAN, AND OTHER SERMONS. Fourth Edition. Crown 8vo. 6s.

"*Ability, eloquence, scholarship, and practical usefulness, are in these Sermons combined in a very unusual degree.*"—British Quarterly.

THE WITNESS OF HISTORY TO CHRIST. Being the Hulsean Lectures for 1870. Sixth Edition. Crown 8vo. 5s.

The following are the subjects of the Five Lectures:—I. " The Antecedent Credibility of the Miraculous." II. " The Adequacy of the Gospel Records." III. " The Victories of Christianity." IV. "Christianity and the Individual." V. "Christianity and the Race." The subjects of the four Appendices are:—A. " The Diversity of Christian Evidences." B. "Confucius." C. "Buddha." D. " Comte."

SEEKERS AFTER GOD. The Lives of Seneca, Epictetus, and Marcus Aurelius. Eighth Edition. Crown 8vo. 6s.

"*A very interesting and valuable book.*"—Saturday Review.

THE SILENCE AND VOICES OF GOD: University and other Sermons. Fifth Edition. Crown 8vo. 6s.

"*We can most cordially recommend Dr. Farrar's singularly beautiful volume of Sermons...... For beauty of diction, felicity of style, aptness of illustration and earnest loving exhortation, the volume is without its parallel.*"—John Bull. "*They are marked by great ability, by an honesty which does not hesitate to acknowledge difficulties and by an earnestness which commands respect.*"—Pall Mall Gazette.

"IN THE DAYS OF THY YOUTH." Sermons on Practical Subjects, preached at Marlborough College from 1871—76. Sixth Edition. Crown 8vo. 9s.

"*All Dr. Farrar's peculiar charm of style is apparent here, all that care and subtleness of analysis, and an even-added distinctness and clear-*

THEOLOGICAL BOOKS. 11

FARRAR (Rev. F. W.)—*continued.*
ness of moral teaching, which is what every kind of sermon wants, and especially a sermon to boys."—Literary Churchman.

ETERNAL HOPE. Five Sermons preached in Westminster Abbey, in 1876. With Preface, Notes, etc. Contents: What Heaven is.—Is Life Worth Living?—'Hell,' What it is not.—Are there few that be saved?—Earthly and Future Consequences of Sin. Eighteenth Thousand. Crown 8vo. 6s.

SAINTLY WORKERS. Lenten Lectures delivered in St. Andrew's, Holborn, March and April, 1878. Third Edition. Crown 8vo. 6s.

EPHPHATHA; or the Amelioration of the World. Sermons preached at Westminster Abbey. With Two Sermons at St. Margaret's, Westminster, on the Opening of Parliament. Crown 8vo. 6s.

MERCY AND JUDGMENT. A Few Last Words on Christian Eschatology, with reference to Dr. Pusey's "What is of Faith?" Crown 8vo. 10s. 6d.

This volume contains a further development of the doctrines propounded in Canon Farrar's former work on 'Eternal Hope,' dealing in full with the objections that have been raised to the validity of those doctrines. \ *It is, therefore, an indispensable companion to the previous volume.*

Fellowship: LETTERS ADDRESSED TO MY SISTER MOURNERS. Fcap. 8vo, cloth gilt. 3s. 6d.

Ferrar.—A COLLECTION OF FOUR IMPORTANT MSS. OF THE GOSPELS, viz., 13, 69, 124, 346, with a view to prove their common origin, and to restore the Text of their Archetype. By the late W. H. FERRAR, M.A., Professor of Latin in the University of Dublin. Edited by T. K. ABBOTT, M.A., Professor of Biblical Greek, Dublin. 4to, half morocco. 10s. 6d.

Forbes.—Works by GRANVILLE H. FORBES, Rector of Broughton:

THE VOICE OF GOD IN THE PSALMS. Cr. 8vo. 6s. 6d.

VILLAGE SERMONS. By a Northamptonshire Rector. Crown 8vo. 6s.

"Such a volume as the present . . . is as great an accession to the cause of a deep theology as the most refined exposition of its fundamental principles. . . . It is part of the beauty of these sermons that while they apply the old truth to the new modes of feeling they seem to preserve the whiteness of its simplicity . . . . There will be plenty of critics to

accuse this volume of inadequacy of doctrine because it says no more than Scripture about vicarious suffering and external retribution. For ourselves we welcome it most cordially as expressing adequately what we believe to be the true burden of the Gospel in a manner which may take hold either of the least or the most cultivated intellect."—Spectator.

Gaskoin.—CHILDREN'S TREASURY OF BIBLE STORIES. By Mrs. HERMAN GASKOIN. Edited, with Preface, by the Rev. G. F. MACLEAR, D.D.
PART I.—Old Testament. 18mo. 1s.
PART II.—New Testament. 18mo. 1s.
PART III.—The Apostles. 18mo. 1s.

"*This very careful and well-written work is as good an introduction to Biblical History as we remember to have come across.*"—Educational Times.

Hardwick.—Works by the Ven. ARCHDEACON HARDWICK:
CHRIST AND OTHER MASTERS. A Historical Inquiry into some of the Chief Parallelisms and Contrasts between Christianity and the Religious Systems of the Ancient World. New Edition, revised, and a Prefatory Memoir by the Rev. FRANCIS PROCTER, M.A. New Edition. Crown 8vo. 10s. 6d.

A HISTORY OF THE CHRISTIAN CHURCH. Middle Age. From Gregory the Great to the Excommunication of Luther. Edited by WILLIAM STUBBS, M.A., Regius Professor of Modern History in the University of Oxford. With Four Maps constructed for this work by A. KEITH JOHNSTON. New Edition. Crown 8vo. 10s. 6d.

"*As a Manual for the student of ecclesiastical history in the Middle Ages, we know no English work which can be compared to Mr. Hardwick's book.*"—Guardian.

A HISTORY of the CHRISTIAN CHURCH DURING THE REFORMATION. New Edition, revised by Professor STUBBS. Crown 8vo. 10s. 6d.

This volume is intended as a sequel and companion to the 'History of the Christian Church during the Middle Age.'

Hare.—Works by the late ARCHDEACON HARE:
THE VICTORY OF FAITH. By JULIUS CHARLES HARE, M.A., Archdeacon of Lewes. Edited by Prof. PLUMPTRE. With Introductory Notices by the late Prof. MAURICE and Dean STANLEY. Third Edition. Crown 8vo. 6s. 6d.

THE MISSION OF THE COMFORTER. With Notes. New Edition, edited by Prof. E. H. PLUMPTRE. Crn. 8vo. 7s. 6d.

THEOLOGICAL BOOKS.

Harper.—THE METAPHYSICS OF THE SCHOOL. By Thomas Harper, S.J. In 5 vols. Vols. I. and II., 8vo. 18s. each.

"*If the Clergy of either communion in this country could be brought to study Father Harper's book, we should augur well for a sounder theology even in the next generation.*"—Church Quarterly Review.

Harris.—SERMONS. By the late GEORGE COLLYER HARRIS, Prebendary of Exeter, and Vicar of St. Luke's, Torquay. With Memoir by CHARLOTTE M. YONGE, and Portrait. Extra fcap. 8vo. 6s.

Hervey.—THE GENEALOGIES OF OUR LORD AND SAVIOUR JESUS CHRIST, as contained in the Gospels of St. Matthew and St. Luke, reconciled with each other, and shown to be in harmony with the true Chronology of the Times. By Lord ARTHUR HERVEY, Bishop of Bath and Wells. 8vo. 10s. 6d.

Hort.—TWO DISSERTATIONS. I. On MONOΓENHΣ ΘEOΣ in Scripture and Tradition. II. On the "Constantinopolitan" Creed and other Eastern Creeds of the Fourth Century. By F. J. A. HORT, D.D., Fellow and Divinity Lecturer of Emmanuel College, Cambridge. 8vo. 7s. 6d.

Howson (Dean)—Works by:

BEFORE THE TABLE. An Inquiry, Historical and Theological, into the True Meaning of the Consecration Rubric in the Communion Service of the Church of England. By the Very Rev. J. S. HOWSON, D.D., Dean of Chester. With an Appendix and Supplement containing Papers by the Right Rev. the Bishop of St. Andrew's and the Rev. R. W. KENNION, .A. 8vo. 7s. 6d.

THE POSITION OF THE PRIEST DURING CONSECRATION IN THE ENGLISH COMMUNION SERVICE. A Supplement and a Reply. Crown 8vo. 2s. 6d.

Hughes.—THE MANLINESS OF CHRIST. By THOMAS HUGHES, Author of 'Tom Brown's School Days.' Cr. 8vo. 4s. 6d.

"*He has given to the world a volume, which so truly, and in some places so picturesquely and strikingly, represents the life of our Lord, that we can only express the hope that it may find its way into the hands of thousands of English working men.*"—Spectator.

Hutton.—ESSAYS: THEOLOGICAL AND LITERARY. By RICHARD HUTTON, .A. New and cheaper issue. 2 vols. 8vo. 18s.

Hymni Ecclesiæ.—Fcap. 8vo. 7s. 6d.

This collection was edited by Dr. Newman while he lived at Oxford.

THEOLOGICAL BOOKS.

Hyacinthe.—CATHOLIC REFORM. By FATHER HYACINTHE. Letters, Fragments, Discourses. Translated by Madame HYACINTHE-LOYSON. With a Preface by the Very Rev. A. P. STANLEY, D.D., Dean of Westminster. Cr. 8vo. 7s. 6d.

"*A valuable contribution to the religious literature of the day.*"—Daily Telegraph.

Illingworth.—SERMONS preached in a College Chapel. With an Appendix. By J. R. Illingworth, M.A., Fellow of Jesus College, and Tutor of Keble College, Oxford. Crown 8vo. 5s.

"*These sermons have a rare intensity and reality of tone. . . . It is full of strength, and we should be glad to induce any one to read it.*"—Spectator.

Imitation of Christ.—FOUR BOOKS. Translated from the Latin, with Preface by the Rev. W. BENHAM, B.D., Vicar of Margate. Printed with Borders in the Ancient Style after Holbein, Dürer, and other Old Masters. Containing Dances of Death, Acts of Mercy, Emblems, and a variety of curious ornamentation. Cr. 8vo, gilt edges. 7s. 6d.

Also in Latin, uniform with the above. New Edition. 7s. 6d.

Jacob.—BUILDING IN SILENCE, AND OTHER SERMONS. By J. A. JACOB, M.A., Minister of St. Thomas's, Paddington. Extra fcap. 8vo. 6s.

Jellett.—THE EFFICACY OF PRAYER: being the Donnellan Lectures for 1877. By J. H. JELLETT, B.D., Senior Fellow of Trinity College, Dublin, formerly President of the Royal Irish Academy. Second Edition. 8vo. 5s.

Jennings and Lowe.—THE PSALMS, with Introductions and Critical Notes. By A. C. JENNINGS, B.A., Jesus College, Cambridge, Tyrwhitt Scholar, Crosse Scholar, Hebrew University Scholar, and Fry Scholar of St. John's College; helped in parts by W. H. LOWE, M.A., Hebrew Lecturer and late Scholar of Christ's College, Cambridge, and Tyrwhitt Scholar. Complete in two vols. crown 8vo. 10s. 6d. each. Vol. 1, Psalms i.—lxxii., with Prolegomena; Vol. 2, Psalms lxxiii.—cl.

Killen.—THE ECCLESIASTICAL HISTORY OF IRELAND from the Earliest Period to the Present Time. By W. D. KILLEN, D.D., President of Assembly's College, Belfast, and Professor of Ecclesiastical History. Two vols. 8vo. 25s.

"*Those who have the leisure will do well to read these two volumes. They are full of interest, and are the result of great research.*"—Spectator.

THEOLOGICAL BOOKS. 15

Kingsley.—Works by the late Rev. CHARLES KINGSLEY, M.A., Rector of Eversley, and Canon of Westminster:

THE WATER OF LIFE, AND OTHER SERMONS. New Edition. Crown 8vo. 6s.

THE GOSPEL OF THE PENTATEUCH; AND DAVID. New Edition. Crown. 8vo. 6s.

GOOD NEWS OF GOD. New Edition. Crown 8vo. 6s.

SERMONS FOR THE TIMES. New Edition. Crown 8vo. 6s.

VILLAGE AND TOWN AND COUNTRY SERMONS. New Edition. Crown 8vo. 6s.

SERMONS on NATIONAL SUBJECTS, THE KING OF THE EARTH, AND OTHER SERMONS. New Edition. Crn. 8vo. 6s.

DISCIPLINE, AND OTHER SERMONS. New Edition. Crown 8vo. 6s.

WESTMINSTER SERMONS. With Preface. New Edition. Crown 8vo. 6s.

OUT OF THE DEEP. Words for the Sorrowful. From the Writings of CHARLES KINGSLEY. Extra fcap. 8vo. 3s. 6d.

Kynaston.—SERMONS PREACHED IN THE COLLEGE CHAPEL, CHELTENHAM, during the First Year of his Office. By the Rev. HERBERT KYNASTON, M.A., Principal of Cheltenham College. Crown 8vo. 6s.

Lightfoot.—Works by J. B. LIGHTFOOT, D.D., Bishop of Durham:

ST. PAUL'S EPISTLE TO THE GALATIANS. A Revised Text, with Introduction, Notes, and Dissertations. Seventh Edition, revised. 8vo, cloth. 12s.

While the Author's object has been to make this commentary generally complete, he has paid special attention to everything relating to St. Paul's personal history and his intercourse with the Apostles and Church of the Circumcision, as it is this feature in the Epistle to the Galatians which has given it an overwhelming interest in recent theological controversy. The Spectator *says—" There is no commentator at once of sounder judgment and more liberal than Dr. Lightfoot."*

ST. PAUL'S EPISTLE TO THE PHILIPPIANS. A Revised Text, with Introduction, Notes, and Dissertations. Sixth Edition, revised. 8vo. 12s.

LIGHTFOOT (Dr.)—*continued.*

"No commentary in the English language can be compared with it in regard to fulness of information, exact scholarship, and laboured attempts to settle everything about the epistle on a solid foundation."—Athenæum.

ST. PAUL'S EPISTLES TO THE COLOSSIANS AND TO PHILEMON. A Revised Text with Introduction, Notes, etc. Fifth Edition, revised. 8vo. 12s.

"It bears marks of continued and extended reading and research, and of ampler materials at command. Indeed, it leaves nothing to be desired by those who seek to study thoroughly the epistles contained in it, and to do so with all known advantages presented in sufficient detail and in convenient form."—Guardian.

ST. CLEMENT OF ROME. An Appendix containing the newly discovered portions of the two Epistles to the Corinthians, with Introductions and Notes, and a Translation of the whole. 8vo. 8s. 6d.

ON A FRESH REVISION OF THE ENGLISH NEW TESTAMENT. Second Edition. Crown 8vo. 6s.

The Author shews in detail the necessity for a fresh revision of the authorized version on the following grounds:—1. *False Readings.* 2. *Artificial distinctions created.* 3. *Real distinctions obliterated.* 4. *Faults of Grammar.* 5. *Faults of Lexicography.* 6. *Treatment of Proper Names, official titles, etc.* 7. *Archaisms, defects in the English, errors of the press, etc.* "*The book is marked by careful scholarship, familiarity with the subject, sobriety, and circumspection.*"—Athenæum.

Maclaren.—SERMONS PREACHED at MANCHESTER. By ALEXANDER MACLAREN. Sixth Edition. Fcap. 8vo. 4s. 6d.

These Sermons represent no special school, but deal with the broad principles of Christian truth, especially in their bearing on practical, every-day life. A few of the titles are:—"*The Stone of Stumbling,*" "*Love and Forgiveness,*" "*The Living Dead,*" "*Memory in Another World,*" *Faith in Christ,*" "*Love and Fear,*" "*The Choice of Wisdom,*" "*The Food of the World.*"

A SECOND SERIES OF SERMONS. Fourth Edition. Fcap. 8vo. 4s. 6d.

The Spectator *characterises them as "vigorous in style, full of thought, rich in illustration, and in an unusual degree interesting."*

A THIRD SERIES OF SERMONS. Third Edition. Fcap. 8vo. 4s. 6d.

MACLAREN (A.)—*continued.*

"*Sermons more sober and yet more forcible, and with a certain wise and practical spirituality about them it would not be easy to find.*"—Spectator.

WEEK-DAY EVENING ADDRESSES. Delivered in Manchester. Extra Fcap. 8vo. 2s. 6d.

Maclear.—Works by the Rev. G. F. MACLEAR, D.D., Warden of St. Augustine's, Canterbury, late Head Master of King's College School:

A CLASS-BOOK OF OLD TESTAMENT HISTORY. With Four Maps. New Edition. 18mo. 4s. 6d.

"*The present volume,*" says the Preface, "*forms a Class-Book of Old Testament History from the Earliest Times to those of Ezra and Nehemiah. In its preparation the most recent authorities have been consulted, and wherever it has appeared useful, Notes have been subjoined illustrative of the Text, and, for the sake of more advanced students, references added to larger works. The Index has been so arranged as to form a concise Dictionary of the Persons and Places mentioned in the course of the Narrative.*" *The Maps, prepared by Stanford, materially add to the value and usefulness of the book.* The British Quarterly Review *calls it* "*A careful and elaborate, though brief compendium of all that modern research has done for the illustration of the Old Testament. We know of no work which contains so much important information in so small a compass.*"

A CLASS-BOOK OF NEW TESTAMENT HISTORY. Including the Connexion of the Old and New Testament. New Edition. 18mo. 5s. 6d.

The present volume forms a sequel to the Author's Class-Book of Old Testament History, and continues the narrative to the close of St. Paul's second imprisonment at Rome. The work is divided into three Books—I. The Connexion between the Old and New Testament. II. The Gospel History. III. The Apostolic History. In the Appendix are given Chronological Tables. The Clerical Journal *says*, "*It is not often that such an amount of useful and interesting matter on biblical subjects is found in so convenient and small a compass as in this well-arranged volume.*"

A CLASS-BOOK OF THE CATECHISM OF THE CHURCH OF ENGLAND. New and Cheaper Edition. 18mo. 1s. 6d.

The present work is intended as a sequel to the two preceding books. "*Like them, it is furnished with notes and references to larger works, and it is hoped that it may be found, especially in the higher forms of our*

THEOLOGICAL BOOKS.

MACLEAR (Dr. G. F.)—*continued.*

Public Schools, to supply a suitable manual of instruction in the chief doctrines of our Church, and a useful help in the preparation of Candidates for Confirmation." The Literary Churchman *says, "It is indeed the work of a scholar and divine, and as such, though extremely simple, it is also extremely instructive. There are few clergy who would not find it useful in preparing Candidates for Confirmation; and there are not a few who would find it useful to themselves as well."*

A FIRST CLASS-BOOK OF THE CATECHISM OF THE CHURCH OF ENGLAND, with Scripture Proofs for Junior Classes and Schools. New Edition. 18mo. 6*d.*

This is an epitome of the larger Class-book, meant for junior students and elementary classes. The book has been carefully condensed, so as to contain clearly and fully the most important part of the contents of the larger book.

A SHILLING-BOOK of OLD TESTAMENT HISTORY. New Edition. 18mo.

This Manual bears the same relation to the larger Old Testament History, that the book just mentioned does to the larger work on the Catechism. It consists of Ten Books, divided into short chapters, and subdivided into sections, each section treating of a single episode in the history, the title of which is given in bold type.

A SHILLING-BOOK of NEW TESTAMENT HISTORY. New Edition. 18mo.

A MANUAL OF INSTRUCTION FOR CONFIRMATION AND FIRST COMMUNION, with Prayers and Devotions. 32mo. 2*s.*

This is an enlarged and improved edition of 'The Order of Confirmation.' To it have been added the Communion Office, with Notes and Explanations, together with a brief form of Self-Examination and Devotions selected from the works of Cosin, Ken, Wilson, and others.

THE ORDER OF CONFIRMATION, with Prayers and Devotions. 32mo. 6*d.*

THE FIRST COMMUNION, with Prayers and Devotions for the Newly Confirmed. 32mo. 6*d.*

THE HOUR OF SORROW; or, The Order for the Burial of the Dead. With Prayers and Hymns. 32mo. 2*s.*

THEOLOGICAL BOOKS. 19

MACLEAR (Dr. G. F.)—*continued.*
APOSTLES OF MEDIÆVAL EUROPE. Cr. 8vo. 4s. 6d.
"*Mr. Maclear will have done a great work if his admirable little volume shall help to break up the dense ignorance which is still prevailing among people at large.*"—Literary Churchman.

Macmillan.—Works by the Rev. HUGH MACMILLAN, LL.D., F.R.S.E. (For other Works by the same Author, see CATALOGUE OF TRAVELS and SCIENTIFIC CATALOGUE).

TWO WORLDS ARE OURS. Globe 8vo. 6s.

THE TRUE VINE; or, the Analogies of our Lord's Allegory. Third Edition. Globe 8vo. 6s.

The Nonconformist *says*—"*It abounds in exquisite bits of description, and in striking facts clearly stated.*" *The* British Quarterly *says*—"*Readers and preachers who are unscientific will find many of his illustrations as valuable as they are beautiful.*"

BIBLE TEACHINGS IN NATURE. Twelfth Edition. Globe 8vo. 6s.

In this volume the author has endeavoured to shew that the teaching of Nature and the teaching of the Bible are directed to the same great end; that the Bible contains the spiritual truths which are necessary to make us wise unto salvation, and the objects and scenes of Nature are the pictures by which these truths are illustrated. "He has made the world more beautiful to us, and unsealed our ears to voices of praise and messages of love that might otherwise have been unheard."—British Quarterly Review. "*Dr. Macmillan has produced a book which may be fitly described as one of the happiest efforts for enlisting physical science in the direct service of religion.*"—Guardian.

THE SABBATH OF THE FIELDS. A Sequel to 'Bible Teachings in Nature.' Second Edition. Globe 8vo. 6s.

"*This volume, like all Dr. Macmillan's productions, is very delightful reading, and of a special kind. Imagination, natural science, and religious instruction are blended together in a very charming way.*"—British Quarterly Review.

THE MINISTRY OF NATURE. Fourth Edition. Globe 8vo. 6s.

"*Whether the reader agree or not with his conclusions, he will acknowledge he is in the presence of an original and thoughtful writer.*"—Pall Mall Gazette. "*There is no class of educated men and women that will not profit by these essays.*"—Standard.

OUR LORD'S THREE RAISINGS FROM THE DEAD. Globe 8vo. 6s.

Materialism: Ancient and Modern. By a late Fellow of Trinity College, Cambridge. Crown 8vo. 2s.

Maurice.—Works by the late Rev. F. DENISON MAURICE, M.A., Professor of Moral Philosophy in the University of Cambridge:

The Spectator *says—"Few of those of our own generation whose names will live in English history or literature have exerted so profound and so permanent an influence as Mr. Maurice."*

THE PATRIARCHS AND LAWGIVERS OF THE OLD TESTAMENT. Third and Cheaper Edition. Crown 8vo. 5s.

The Nineteen Discourses contained in this volume were preached in the chapel of Lincoln's Inn during the year 1851.

THE PROPHETS AND KINGS OF THE OLD TESTAMENT. New Edition. Crown 8vo. 10s. 6d.

Mr. Maurice, in the spirit which animated the compilers of the Church Lessons, has in these Sermons regarded the Prophets more as preachers of righteousness than as mere predictors—an aspect of their lives which, he thinks, has been greatly overlooked in our day, and than which there is none we have more need to contemplate. He has found that the Old Testament Prophets, taken in their simple natural sense, clear up many of the difficulties which beset us in the daily work of life; make the past intelligible, the present endurable, and the future real and hopeful.

THE GOSPEL OF THE KINGDOM OF HEAVEN. A Series of Lectures on the Gospel of St. Luke. New Edition. Crown 8vo. 9s.

Mr. Maurice, in his Preface to these Twenty-eight Lectures, says— "In these Lectures I have endeavoured to ascertain what is told us respecting the life of Jesus by one of those Evangelists who proclaim Him to be the Christ, who says that He did come from a Father, that He did baptize with the Holy Spirit, that He did rise from the dead. I have chosen the one who is most directly connected with the later history of the Church, who was not an Apostle, who professedly wrote for the use of a man already instructed in the faith of the Apostles. I have followed the course of the writer's narrative, not changing it under any pretext. I have adhered to his phraseology, striving to avoid the substitution of any other for his."

THE GOSPEL OF ST. JOHN. A Series of Discourses. New Edition. Crown 8vo. 6s.

THEOLOGICAL BOOKS.

MAURICE (Rev. F. D.)—*continued.*

The Literary Churchman *thus speaks of this volume:* "*Thorough honesty, reverence, and deep thought pervade the work, which is every way solid and philosophical, as well as theological, and abounding with suggestions which the patient student may draw out more at length for himself.*"

THE EPISTLES OF ST. JOHN. A Series of Lectures on Christian Ethics. Second and Cheaper Edition. Cr. 8vo. 6s.

These Lectures on Christian Ethics were delivered to the students of the Working Men's College, Great Ormond Street, London, on a series of Sunday mornings. Mr. Maurice believes that the question in which we are most interested, the question which most affects our studies and our daily lives, is the question, whether there is a foundation for human morality, or whether it is dependent upon the opinions and fashions of different ages and countries. This important question will be found amply and fairly discussed in this volume, which the National Review *calls* "*Mr. Maurice's most effective and instructive work. He is peculiarly fitted by the constitution of his mind, to throw light on St. John's writings.*" *Appended is a note on 'Positivism and its Teacher.'*

EXPOSITORY SERMONS ON THE PRAYER-BOOK. The Prayer-book considered especially in reference to the Romish System; and the Lord's Prayer. Crown 8vo. 9s.

After an Introductory Sermon, Mr. Maurice goes over the various parts of the Church Service, expounds in eighteen Sermons their intention and significance, and shews how appropriate they are as expressions of the deepest longings and wants of all classes of men.

WHAT IS REVELATION? A Series of Sermons on the Epiphany; to which are added, Letters to a Theological Student on the Bampton Lectures of Mr. Mansel. Crown 8vo. 10s. 6d.

Both Sermons and Letters were called forth by the doctrine maintained by Mr. Mansel in his Bampton Lectures, that Revelation cannot be a direct Manifestation of the Infinite Nature of God. Mr. Maurice maintains the opposite doctrine, and in his Sermons explains why, in spite of the high authorities on the other side, he must still assert the principle which he discovers in the Services of the Church and throughout the Bible.

SEQUEL TO THE INQUIRY, 'WHAT IS REVELATION?' Letters in Reply to Mr. Mansel's Examination of 'Strictures on the Bampton Lectures.' Crown 8vo. 6s.

This, as the title indicates, was called forth by Mr. Mansel's examination of Mr. Maurice's Strictures on his doctrine of the Infinite.

THEOLOGICAL BOOKS.

MAURICE (Rev. F. D.)—*continued.*

THEOLOGICAL ESSAYS. Third Edition. Crown 8vo. 10s. 6d.

"*The book,*" *says Mr. Maurice, "expresses thoughts which have been working in my mind for years; the method of it has not been adopted carelessly; even the composition has undergone frequent revision.*"

THE DOCTRINE OF SACRIFICE DEDUCED FROM THE SCRIPTURES. New Edition. Crown 8vo. 7s. 6d.

THE RELIGIONS OF THE WORLD, AND THEIR RELATIONS TO CHRISTIANITY. Fifth Edition. Crown 8vo. 5s.

ON THE SABBATH DAY; the Character of the Warrior, and on the Interpretation of History. Fcap. 8vo. 2s. 6d.

THE LORD'S PRAYER, THE CREED, AND THE COMMANDMENTS. A Manual for Parents and Schoolmasters. To which is added the Order of the Scriptures. 18mo, cloth limp. 1s.

DIALOGUES ON FAMILY WORSHIP. Crown 8vo. 6s.

SOCIAL MORALITY. Twenty-one Lectures delivered in the University of Cambridge. New and Cheaper Edition. Cr. 8vo. 10s. 6d.

"*Whilst reading it we are charmed by the freedom from exclusiveness and prejudice, the large charity, the loftiness of thought, the eagerness to recognise and appreciate whatever there is of real worth extant in the world, which animates it from one end to the other. We gain new thoughts and new ways of viewing things, even more, perhaps, from being brought for a time under the influence of so noble and spiritual a mind.*"
—Athenæum.

THE CONSCIENCE: Lectures on Casuistry, delivered in the University of Cambridge. Second and Cheaper Edition. Crown 8vo. 5s.

The Saturday Review *says*—"*We rise from the perusal of these lectures with a detestation of all that is selfish and mean, and with a living impression that there is such a thing as goodness after all.*"

LECTURES ON THE ECCLESIASTICAL HISTORY OF THE FIRST AND SECOND CENTURIES. 8vo. 10s. 6d.

THEOLOGICAL BOOKS. 23

MAURICE (Rev. F. D.)—*continued.*

LEARNING AND WORKING. Six Lectures delivered in Willis's Rooms, London, in June and July, 1854.—THE RELIGION OF ROME, and its Influence on Modern Civilisation. Four Lectures delivered in the Philosophical Institution of Edinburgh, in December, 1854. Crown 8vo. 5s.

SERMONS PREACHED IN COUNTRY CHURCHES. New Edition. Crown 8vo. 10s. 6d.

"*Earnest, practical, and extremely simple.*"—Literary Churchman. "*Good specimens of his simple and earnest eloquence. The Gospel incidents are realized with a vividness which we can well believe made the common people hear him gladly. Moreover, they are sermons which must have done the hearers good.*"—John Bull.

Milligan.—THE RESURRECTION OF OUR LORD. The Croall Lecture for 1879—80. By the Rev. Professor MILLIGAN, D.D., Professor of Divinity and Biblical Criticism in the University of Aberdeen. 8vo. 9s.

Moorhouse.—Works by JAMES MOORHOUSE, M.A., Bishop of Melbourne :

SOME MODERN DIFFICULTIES RESPECTING the FACTS OF NATURE AND REVELATION. Fcap. 8vo. 2s. 6d.

JACOB. Three Sermons preached before the University of Cambridge in Lent, 1870. Extra fcap. 8vo. 3s. 6d.

O'Brien.—PRAYER. Five Sermons preached in the Chapel of Trinity College, Dublin. By JAMES THOMAS O'BRIEN, D.D., Bishop of Ossory and Ferns. 8vo. 6s.

Palgrave.—HYMNS. By FRANCIS TURNER PALGRAVE. Third Edition, enlarged. 18mo. 1s. 6d.

This is a collection of twenty original Hymns, which the Literary Churchman *speaks of as "so choice, so perfect, and so refined,—so tender in feeling, and so scholarly in expression."*

Paul of Tarsus. An Inquiry into the Times and the Gospel of the Apostle of the Gentiles. By a GRADUATE. 8vo. 10s. 6d.

"*Turn where we will throughout the volume, we find the best fruit of patient inquiry, sound scholarship, logical argument, and fairness of conclusion. No thoughtful reader will rise from its perusal without a real and lasting profit to himself, and a sense of permanent addition to the cause of truth.*"—Standard.

THEOLOGICAL BOOKS.

Philochristus.—MEMOIRS OF A DISCIPLE OF THE LORD. Second Edition. 8vo. 12s.

"*The winning beauty of this book and the fascinating power with which the subject of it appeals to all English minds will secure for it many readers.*"—Contemporary Review.

Picton.—THE MYSTERY OF MATTER; and other Essays. By J. ALLANSON PICTON, Author of 'New Theories and the Old Faith.' Cheaper Edition. With New Preface. Crown 8vo. 6s.

Contents—The Mystery of Matter: The Philosophy of Ignorance: The Antithesis of Faith and Sight: The Essential Nature of Religion: Christian Pantheism.

Plumptre.—MOVEMENTS IN RELIGIOUS THOUGHT. Sermons preached before the University of Cambridge, Lent Term, 1879. By E. H. PLUMPTRE, D.D., Professor of Divinity, King's College, London, Prebendary of St. Paul's, etc. Fcap. 8vo. 3s. 6d.

Prescott.—THE THREEFOLD CORD. Sermons preached before the University of Cambridge. By J. E. PRESCOTT, B.D. Fcap. 8vo. 3s. 6d.

Procter.—A HISTORY OF THE BOOK OF COMMON PRAYER: With a Rationale of its Offices. By FRANCIS PROCTER, M.A. Fifteenth Edition, revised and enlarged. Cr. 8vo. 10s. 6d.

The Athenæum *says—"The origin of every part of the Prayer-book has been diligently investigated,—and there are few questions or facts connected with it which are not either sufficiently explained, or so referred to that persons interested may work out the truth for themselves."*

Procter and Maclear.—AN ELEMENTARY INTRODUCTION TO THE BOOK OF COMMON PRAYER. Re-arranged and Supplemented by an Explanation of the Morning and Evening Prayer and the Litany. By F. PROCTER, M.A., and G. F. MACLEAR, D.D. New Edition. Enlarged by the addition of the Communion Service and the Baptismal and Confirmation Offices. 18mo. 2s. 6d.

The Literary Churchman *characterises it as "by far the completest and most satisfactory book of its kind we know. We wish it were in the hands of every schoolboy and every schoolmaster in the kingdom."*

Psalms of David CHRONOLOGICALLY ARRANGED An Amended Version, with Historical Introductions and Explanatory Notes. By FOUR FRIENDS. Second and Cheaper Edition, much enlarged. Crown 8vo. 8s. 6d.

One of the chief designs of the Editors, in preparing this volume, was to restore the Psalter as far as possible to the order in which the Psalms were written. They give the division of each Psalm into strophes, and of each strophe into the lines which composed it, and amend the errors of translation. The Spectator *calls it "one of the most instructive and valuable books that have been published for many years."*

Psalter (Golden Treasury).—THE STUDENT'S EDITION. Being an Edition of the above with briefer Notes. 18mo. 3s. 6d.

The aim of this edition is simply to put the reader as far as possible in possession of the plain meaning of the writer. "It is a gem," the Nonconformist *says.*

Pulsford.—SERMONS PREACHED IN TRINITY CHURCH, GLASGOW. By WILLIAM PULSFORD, D.D. Cheaper Edition. Crown 8vo. 4s. 6d.

Ramsay.—THE CATECHISER'S MANUAL; or, the Church Catechism Illustrated and Explained, for the Use of Clergymen, Schoolmasters, and Teachers. By ARTHUR RAMSAY, M.A. Second Edition. 18mo. 1s. 6d.

Rays of Sunlight for Dark Days. A Book of Selections for the Suffering. With a Preface by C. J. VAUGHAN, D.D. 18mo. Eighth Edition. 3s. 6d. Also in morocco, old style.

Dr. Vaughan says in the Preface, after speaking of the general run of Books of Comfort for Mourners—"It is because I think that the little volume now offered to the Christian sufferer is one of greater wisdom and of deeper experience, that I have readily consented to the request that I would introduce it by a few words of Preface." The book consists of a series of very brief extracts from a great variety of authors, in prose and poetry, suited to the many moods of a mourning or suffering mind. "Mostly gems of the first water."—Clerical Journal.

Reynolds.—NOTES OF THE CHRISTIAN LIFE. A Selection of Sermons by HENRY ROBERT REYNOLDS, B.A., President of Cheshunt College, and Fellow of University College, London. Crown 8vo. 7s. 6d.

Roberts.—DISCUSSIONS ON THE GOSPELS. By the Rev. ALEXANDER ROBERTS, D.D. Second Edition, revised and enlarged. 8vo. 16s.

Robinson.—MAN IN THE IMAGE OF GOD; and other Sermons preached in the Chapel of the Magdalen, Streatham, 1874—76. By H. G. ROBINSON, M.A., Prebendary of York. Crown 8vo. 7s. 6d.

THEOLOGICAL BOOKS.

Romanes.—CHRISTIAN PRAYER AND GENERAL LAWS, being the Burney Prize Essay for 1873. With an Appendix, examining the views of Messrs. Knight, Robertson, Brooke, Tyndall, and Galton. By GEORGE J. ROMANES, M.A. Crown 8vo. 5s.

Rushbrooke.—SYNOPTICON: An Exposition of the Common Matter of the Synoptic Gospels. By W. G. RUSHBROOKE, M.L., Fellow of St. John's College, Cambridge. Printed in colours. In Six Parts and Appendices. 4to. Part I. 3s. 6d. Parts II. and III. 7s. Parts IV. V. and VI. With Indices. 10s. 6d. Appendices, 10s. 6d., or the complete work, in one vol. cloth, 35s.

Salmon.—NON-MIRACULOUS CHRISTIANITY, and other Sermons, preached in the Chapel of Trinity College, Dublin. By GEORGE SALMON, D.D., Chancellor of St. Patrick's Cathedral, and Regius Professor of Divinity in the University of Dublin. Crown 8vo. 6s.

Sanday.—THE GOSPELS IN THE SECOND CENTURY. An Examination of the Critical part of a Work entitled 'Supernatural Religion.' By WILLIAM SANDAY, M.A., late Fellow of Trinity College, Oxford. Crown 8vo. 8s. 6d.

Scotch Sermons, 1880.—By Principal CAIRD; Rev. J. CUNNINGHAM, D.D.; Rev. D. J. FERGUSON, B.D.; Professor WM. KNIGHT, LL.D.; Rev. W. MACKINTOSH, D.D.; Rev. W. L. M'FARLAN; Rev. ALLAN MENZIES, B.D.; Rev. T. NICOLL; Rev. T. RAIN, M.A.; Rev. A. SEMPLE, B.D.; Rev. J. STEVENSON; Rev. PATRICK STEVENSON; Rev. R. H. STORY, D.D. 8vo. Third Edition. 10s. 6d.

The Pall Mall Gazette *says—" The publication of a volume of Scotch Sermons, contributed by members of the Established Church, seems likely to cause as much commotion in that body as 'Essays and Reviews' did in the Church of England."*

Selborne.—THE BOOK OF PRAISE: From the Best English Hymn Writers. Selected and arranged by Lord SELBORNE. With Vignette by T. WOOLNER, R.A. 18mo. 4s. 6d.

It has been the Editor's desire and aim to adhere strictly, in all cases in which it could be ascertained, to the genuine uncorrupted text of the authors themselves. The names of the authors and date of composition of the hymns, when known, are affixed, while notes are added to the volume, giving further details. The Hymns are arranged according to subjects.

THEOLOGICAL BOOKS. 27

SELBORNE (Lord)—*continued.*

"*There is not room for two opinions as to the value of the* 'Book of Praise.'"
—Guardian. "*Approaches as nearly as one can conceive to perfection.*"
—Nonconformist.

BOOK OF PRAISE HYMNAL. *See* end of this Catalogue.

Service.—SALVATION HERE AND HEREAFTER.
Sermons and Essays. By the Rev. JOHN SERVICE, D.D., Minister of Inch. Fourth Edition. Crown 8vo. 6s.

"*We have enjoyed to-day a rare pleasure, having just closed a volume of sermons which rings true metal from title page to finis, and proves that another and very powerful recruit has been added to that small band of ministers of the Gospel who are not only abreast of the religious thought of their time, but have faith enough and courage enough to handle the questions which are the most critical, and stir men's minds most deeply, with frankness and thoroughness.*"—Spectator.

Shipley.—A THEORY ABOUT SIN, in relation to some Facts of Daily Life. Lent Lectures on the Seven Deadly Sins. By the Rev. ORBY SHIPLEY, M.A. Crown 8vo. 7s. 6d.

"*Two things Mr. Shipley has done, and each of them is of considerable worth. He has grouped these sins afresh on a philosophic principle ..... and he has applied the touchstone to the facts of our moral life... so wisely and so searchingly as to constitute his treatise a powerful antidote to self-deception.*"—Literary Churchman.

Smith.—PROPHECY A PREPARATION FOR CHRIST. Eight Lectures preached before the University of Oxford, being the Bampton Lectures for 1869. By R. PAYNE SMITH, D.D., Dean of Canterbury. Second and Cheaper Edition. Crown 8vo. 6s.

The author's object in these Lectures is to shew that there exists in the Old Testament an element, which no criticism on naturalistic principles can either account for or explain away: that element is Prophecy. The author endeavours to prove that its force does not consist merely in its predictions. "*These Lectures overflow with solid learning.*"—Record.

Smith.—CHRISTIAN FAITH. Sermons preached before the University of Cambridge. By W. SAUMAREZ SMITH, M.A., Principal of St. Aidan's College, Birkenhead. Fcap. 8vo. 3s. 6d.

Stanley.—Works by the late Very Rev. A. P. STANLEY, D.D., Dean of Westminster:

THE ATHANASIAN CREED, with a Preface on the General Recommendations of the RITUAL COMMISSION. Cr. 8vo. 2s.

STANLEY (Dean)—*continued*.

"*Dr. Stanley puts with admirable force the objections which may be made to the Creed; equally admirable, we think, in his statement of its advantages.*"—Spectator.

THE NATIONAL THANKSGIVING. Sermons preached in Westminster Abbey. Second Edition. Crown 8vo. 2s. 6d.

ADDRESSES AND SERMONS AT ST. ANDREW'S in 1872, 1875 and 1876. Crown 8vo. 5s.

Stewart and Tait.—THE UNSEEN UNIVERSE; or, Physical Speculations on a Future State. By Professors BALFOUR STEWART and P. G. TAIT. Tenth Edition, Revised and Enlarged. Crown 8vo. 6s.

"*A most remarkable and most interesting volume, which, probably more than any that has appeared in modern times, will affect religious thought on many momentous questions—insensibly it may be, but very largely and very beneficially.*"—Church Quarterly. "*This book is one which well deserves the attention of thoughtful and religious readers...... It is a perfectly safe enquiry, on scientific grounds, into the possibilities of a future existence.*"—Guardian.

Stubbs.—Works by Rev. CHARLES WILLIAM STUBBS, M.A., Vicar of Granborough, Bucks. :

VILLAGE POLITICS. Addresses and Sermons on the Labour Question. Extra fcap. 8vo. 3s. 6d.

"*The sermons in this book are all worth reading. . . . . They are full of warm sympathy for the labourers and sound practical advice to all classes concerned in the struggle.*"—Guardian. "*It is a most encouraging sign of the times, that a clergyman of the Church of England can be found to deliver such discourses as these.*"—Westminster Review.

THE MYTHE OF LIFE, and other Sermons, with an Introduction on the Social Mission of the Church. Extra fcap. 8vo. 3s. 6d.

Taylor.—THE RESTORATION OF BELIEF. New and Revised Edition. By ISAAC TAYLOR, Esq. Crown 8vo. 8s. 6d.

Temple.—SERMONS PREACHED IN THE CHAPEL of RUGBY SCHOOL. By F. TEMPLE, D.D., Bishop of Exeter. New and Cheaper Edition. Extra fcap. 8vo. 4s. 6d.

This volume contains Thirty-five Sermons on topics more or less intimately connected with every-day life. The following are a few of the subjects discoursed upon:—"*Love and Duty;*" "*Coming to Christ;*"

THEOLOGICAL BOOKS.

TEMPLE (Dr.)—*continued.*
"Great Men;" "Faith;" "Doubts;" "Scruples;" "Original Sin;" "Friendship;" "Helping Others;" "The Discipline of Temptation;" "Strength a Duty;" "Worldliness;" "Ill Temper;" "The Burial of the Past."

A SECOND SERIES OF SERMONS PREACHED IN THE CHAPEL OF RUGBY SCHOOL. Second Edition. Extra fcap. 8vo. 6s.

This Second Series of Forty-two brief, pointed, practical Sermons, on topics intimately connected with the every-day life of young and old, will be acceptable to all who are acquainted with the First Series. The following are a few of the subjects treated of:—*"Disobedience," "Almsgiving," "The Unknown Guidance of God," "Apathy one of our Trials," "High Aims in Leaders," "Doing our Best," "The Use of Knowledge," "Use of Observances," "Martha and Mary," "John the Baptist," "Severity before Mercy," "Even Mistakes Punished," "Morality and Religion," "Children," "Action the Test of Spiritual Life," "Self-Respect," "Too Late," "The Tercentenary."*

A THIRD SERIES OF SERMONS PREACHED IN RUGBY SCHOOL CHAPEL IN 1867—1869. Extra fcap. 8vo. 6s.

This Third Series of Bishop Temple's Rugby Sermons, contains thirty-six brief discourses, including the "Good-bye" sermon preached on his leaving Rugby to enter on the office he now holds.

Thornely.—THE ETHICAL AND SOCIAL ASPECT OF HABITUAL CONFESSION TO A PRIEST. By THOMAS THORNELY, B.A., LL.M., Lightfoot and Whewell Scholar in the University of Cambridge, Law Student at Trinity Hall and Inns of Court, Student in Jurisprudence and Roman Law. Crown 8vo. 4s. 6d.

"The calm and judicial spirit in which the inquiry is conducted is in keeping with the aim of the writer, and we are heartily in sympathy with him in his conclusions as far as he goes."—London Quarterly. *"It is marked by an evident desire to avoid over-statement, and to be strictly impartial."*—Cambridge Review.

Thring.—THOUGHTS ON LIFE-SCIENCE. By Rev. EDWARD THRING, M.A. New Edition, enlarged and revised. Crown 8vo. 7s. 6d.

Thrupp.—AN INTRODUCTION TO THE STUDY AND USE OF THE PSALMS. By the Rev. J. F. THRUPP, M.A., late Fellow of Trinity College, Cambridge. New Edition. 2 vols. 8vo. 25s.

Trench.—Works by R. CHENEVIX TRENCH, D.D., Archbishop of Dublin:

NOTES ON THE PARABLES OF OUR LORD. Thirteenth Edition. 8vo. 12s.

This work has taken its place as a standard exposition and interpretation of Christ's Parables. The book is prefaced by an Introductory Essay in four chapters:—I. On the definition of the Parable. II. On Teaching by Parables. III. On the Interpretation of the Parables. IV. On other Parables besides those in the Scriptures. The author then proceeds to take up the Parables one by one, and by the aid of philology, history, antiquities, and the researches of travellers, shews forth the significance, beauty, and applicability of each, concluding with what he deems its true moral interpretation. In the numerous Notes are many valuable references, illustrative quotations, critical and philological annotations, etc., and appended to the volume is a classified list of fifty-six works on the Parables.

NOTES ON THE MIRACLES OF OUR LORD. Eleventh Edition, revised. 8vo. 12s.

In the 'Preliminary Essay' to this work, all the momentous and interesting questions that have been raised in connection with Miracles, are discussed with considerable fulness. The Essay consists of six chapters:— I. On the Names of Miracles, i.e. the Greek words by which they are designated in the New Testament. II. The Miracles and Nature—What is the difference between a Miracle and any event in the ordinary course of Nature? III. The Authority of Miracles—Is the Miracle to command absolute obedience? IV. The Evangelical, compared with the other cycles of Miracles. V. The Assaults on the Miracles—1. The Jewish. 2. The Heathen (Celsus, etc.). 3. The Pantheistic (Spinosa, etc.). 4. The Sceptical (Hume). 5. The Miracles only relatively miraculous (Schleiermacher). 6. The Rationalistic (Paulus). 7. The Historico-Critical (Woolston, Strauss). VI. The Apologetic Worth of the Miracles. The author then treats the separate Miracles as he does the Parables.

SYNONYMS OF THE NEW TESTAMENT. Ninth Edition, enlarged. 8vo. 12s.

This Edition has been carefully revised, and a considerable number of new Synonyms added. Appended is an Index to the Synonyms, and an Index to many other words alluded to or explained throughout the work. "He is," the Athenæum *says, "a guide in this department of knowledge to whom his readers may intrust themselves with confidence. His sober judgment and sound sense are barriers against the misleading influence of arbitrary hypotheses."*

ON THE AUTHORIZED VERSION OF THE NEW TESTAMENT. Second Edition. 8vo. 7s.

After some Introductory Remarks, in which the propriety of a revision is briefly discussed, the whole question of the merits of the present version

THEOLOGICAL BOOKS.

TRENCH (Archbishop)—*continued.*
is gone into in detail, in eleven chapters. Appended is a chronological list of works bearing on the subject, an Index of the principal Texts considered, an Index of Greek Words, and an Index of other Words referred to throughout the book.

STUDIES IN THE GOSPELS. Fourth Edition, revised. 8vo. 10s. 6d.

This book is published under the conviction that the assertion often made is untrue,—viz. that the Gospels are in the main plain and easy, and that all the chief difficulties of the New Testament are to be found in the Epistles. These 'Studies,' sixteen in number, are the fruit of a much larger scheme, and each Study deals with some important episode mentioned in the Gospels, in a critical, philosophical, and practical manner. Many references and quotations are added to the Notes. Among the subjects treated are:—The Temptation; Christ and the Samaritan Woman; The Three Aspirants; The Transfiguration; Zacchæus; The True Vine; The Penitent Malefactor; Christ and the Two Disciples on the way to Emmaus.

COMMENTARY ON THE EPISTLES to the SEVEN CHURCHES IN ASIA. Third Edition, revised. 8vo. 8s. 6d.

The present work consists of an Introduction, being a commentary on Rev. i. 4—20, a detailed examination of each of the Seven Epistles, in all its bearings, and an Excursus on the Historico-Prophetical Interpretation of the Epistles.

THE SERMON ON THE MOUNT. An Exposition drawn from the writings of St. Augustine, with an Essay on his merits as an Interpreter of Holy Scripture. Fourth Edition, enlarged. 8vo. 10s. 6d.

The first half of the present work consists of a dissertation in eight chapters on 'Augustine as an Interpreter of Scripture,' the titles of the several chapters being as follow:—I. Augustine's General Views of Scripture and its Interpretation. II. The External Helps for the Interpretation of Scripture possessed by Augustine. III. Augustine's Principles and Canons of Interpretation. IV. Augustine's Allegorical Interpretation of Scripture. V. Illustrations of Augustine's Skill as an Interpreter of Scripture. VI. Augustine on John the Baptist and on St. Stephen. VII. Augustine on the Epistle to the Romans. VIII. Miscellaneous Examples of Augustine's Interpretation of Scripture. The latter half of the work consists of Augustine's Exposition of the Sermon on the Mount, not however a mere series of quotations from Augustine, but a connected account of his sentiments on the various passages of that Sermon, interspersed with criticisms by Archbishop Trench.

SHIPWRECKS OF FAITH. Three Sermons preached before the University of Cambridge in May, 1867. Fcap. 8vo. 2s. 6d.

TRENCH (Archbishop)—*continued*.

These Sermons are especially addressed to young men. The subjects are "Balaam," "Saul," and "Judas Iscariot," These lives are set forth as beacon-lights, "to warn us off from perilous reefs and quicksands, which have been the destruction of many, and which might only too easily be ours." The John Bull *says—"they are, like all he writes, affectionate and earnest discourses."*

SERMONS Preached for the most part in Ireland. 8vo. 10s. 6d.

This volume consists of Thirty-two Sermons, the greater part of which were preached in Ireland; the subjects are as follow:—Jacob, a Prince with God and with Men—Agrippa—The Woman that was a Sinner—Secret Faults—The Seven Worse Spirits—Freedom in the Truth—Joseph and his Brethren—Bearing one another's Burdens—Christ's Challenge to the World—The Love of Money—The Salt of the Earth—The Armour of God—Light in the Lord—The Jailer of Philippi—The Thorn in the Flesh—Isaiah's Vision—Selfishness—Abraham interceding for Sodom—Vain Thoughts—Pontius Pilate—The Brazen Serpent—The Death and Burial of Moses—A Word from the Cross—The Church's Worship in the Beauty of Holiness—Every Good Gift from Above—On the Hearing of Prayer—The Kingdom which cometh not with Observation—Pressing towards the Mark—Saul—The Good Shepherd—The Valley of Dry Bones—All Saints.

LECTURES ON MEDIEVAL CHURCH HISTORY. Being the Substance of Lectures delivered in Queen's College, London. Second Edition, revised. 8vo. 12s.

Contents:—The Middle Ages Beginning—The Conversion of England—Islam—The Conversion of Germany—The Iconoclasts—The Crusades—The Papacy at its Height—The Sects of the Middle Ages—The Mendicant Orders—The Waldenses—The Revival of Learning—Christian Art in the Middle Ages, &c. &c.

THE HULSEAN LECTURES, 1845-1846. Fifth Edition, revised. 8vo. 7s. 6d.

This volume consists of Sixteen Sermons, eight being on 'The Fitness of Holy Scripture for unfolding the Spiritual Life of Men,' the others on 'Christ, the Desire of all Nations; or, the unconscious Prophecies of Heathendom.'

Tulloch.—THE CHRIST OF THE GOSPELS AND THE CHRIST OF MODERN CRITICISM. Lectures on M. RENAN'S 'Vie de Jésus.' By JOHN TULLOCH, D.D., Principal of the College of St. Mary, in the University of St. Andrew's. Extra fcap. 8vo. 4s. 6d.

Vaughan.—Works by the very Rev. CHARLES JOHN VAUGHAN, D.D., Dean of Llandaff and Master of the Temple:

CHRIST SATISFYING THE INSTINCTS OF HUMANITY. Eight Lectures delivered in the Temple Church. Second Edition. Extra fcap. 8vo. 3s. 6d.

"*We are convinced that there are congregations, in number unmistakably increasing, to whom such Essays as these, full of thought and learning, are infinitely more beneficial, for they are more acceptable, than the recognised type of sermons.*"—John Bull.

THE BOOK AND THE LIFE, and other Sermons, preached before the University of Cambridge. Third Edition. Fcap. 8vo. 4s. 6d.

TWELVE DISCOURSES on SUBJECTS CONNECTED WITH THE LITURGY and WORSHIP of the CHURCH OF ENGLAND. Fourth Edition. Fcap. 8vo. 6s.

LESSONS OF LIFE AND GODLINESS. A Selection of Sermons preached in the Parish Church of Doncaster. Fourth and Cheaper Edition. Fcap. 8vo. 3s. 6d.

This volume consists of Nineteen Sermons, mostly on subjects connected with the every-day walk and conversation of Christians. The Spectator *styles them "earnest and human. They are adapted to every class and order in the social system, and will be read with wakeful interest by all who seek to amend whatever may be amiss in their natural disposition or in their acquired habits."*

WORDS FROM THE GOSPELS. A Second Selection of Sermons preached in the Parish Church of Doncaster. Third Edition. Fcap. 8vo. 4s. 6d.

The Nonconformist *characterises these Sermons as "of practical earnestness, of a thoughtfulness that penetrates the common conditions and experiences of life, and brings the truths and examples of Scripture to bear on them with singular force, and of a style that owes its real elegance to the simplicity and directness which have fine culture for their roots."*

LIFE'S WORK AND GOD'S DISCIPLINE. Three Sermons. Third Edition. Fcap. 8vo. 2s. 6d.

THE WHOLESOME WORDS OF JESUS CHRIST. Four Sermons preached before the University of Cambridge in November, 1866. Second Edition. Fcap. 8vo. 3s. 6d.

Dr. Vaughan uses the word "Wholesome" here in its literal and original sense, the sense in which St. Paul uses it, as meaning healthy, sound, conducing to right living; and in these Sermons he points out and illustrates several of the "wholesome" characteristics of the Gospel, —the Words of Christ. The John Bull *says this volume is "replete with all the author's well-known vigour of thought and richness of expression."*

THEOLOGICAL BOOKS.

VAUGHAN (Dr. C. J.)—*continued.*

FOES OF FAITH. Sermons preached before the University of Cambridge in November, 1868. Second Edition. Fcap. 8vo. 3*s.* 6*d.*

The *"Foes of Faith" preached against in these Four Sermons are:—* I. *"Unreality." II. "Indolence." III. "Irreverence." IV. "Inconsistency."*

LECTURES ON THE EPISTLE to the PHILIPPIANS. Fourth and Cheaper Edition. Extra fcap. 8vo. 5*s.*

Each Lecture is prefaced by a literal translation from the Greek of the paragraph which forms its subject, contains first a minute explanation of the passage on which it is based, and then a practical application of the verse or clause selected as its text.

LECTURES ON THE REVELATION OF ST. JOHN. Fourth Edition. Two Vols. Extra fcap. 8vo. 9*s.*

In this Edition of these Lectures, the literal translations of the passages expounded will be found interwoven in the body of the Lectures themselves. "*Dr. Vaughan's Sermons,*" *the* Spectator *says,* "*are the most practical discourses on the Apocalypse with which we are acquainted.*" *Prefixed is a Synopsis of the Book of Revelation, and appended is an Index of passages illustrating the language of the Book.*

EPIPHANY, LENT, AND EASTER. A Selection of Expository Sermons. Third Edition. Crown 8vo. 10*s.* 6*d.*

THE EPISTLES OF ST. PAUL. For English Readers. PART I., containing the FIRST EPISTLE TO THE THESSALONIANS. Second Edition. 8vo. 1*s.* 6*d.*

It is the object of this work to enable English readers, unacquainted with Greek, to enter with intelligence into the meaning, connexion, and phraseology of the writings of the great Apostle.

ST. PAUL'S EPISTLE TO THE ROMANS. The Greek Text, with English Notes. Fifth Edition. Crown 8vo. 7*s.* 6*d.*

The Guardian *says of the work*—"*For educated young men his commentary seems to fill a gap hitherto unfilled. . . . As a whole, Dr. Vaughan appears to us to have given to the world a valuable book of original and careful and earnest thought bestowed on the accomplishment of a work which will be of much service and which is much needed.*"

THE CHURCH OF THE FIRST DAYS.
 Series I. The Church of Jerusalem. Third Edition.
 ,, II. The Church of the Gentiles. Third Edition.
 ,, III. The Church of the World. Third Edition.
Fcap. 8vo. 4*s.* 6*d.* each.

The British Quarterly *says*—"*These Sermons are worthy of all praise, and are models of pulpit teaching.*"

VAUGHAN (Dr. C. J.)—*continued*.

COUNSELS for YOUNG STUDENTS. Three Sermons preached before the University of Cambridge at the Opening of the Academical Year 1870-71. Fcap. 8vo. 2s. 6d.

NOTES FOR LECTURES ON CONFIRMATION, with suitable Prayers. Eleventh Edition. Fcap. 8vo. 1s. 6d.

THE TWO GREAT TEMPTATIONS. The Temptation of Man, and the Temptation of Christ. Lectures delivered in the Temple Church, Lent 1872. Second Edition. Extra fcap. 8vo. 3s. 6d.

WORDS FROM THE CROSS: Lent Lectures, 1875; and Thoughts for these Times: University Sermons, 1874. Extra fcap. 8vo. 4s. 6d.

ADDRESSES TO YOUNG CLERGYMEN, delivered at Salisbury in September and October, 1875. Extra fcap. 8vo. 4s. 6d.

HEROES OF FAITH: Lectures on Hebrews xi. Extra fcap. 8vo. 6s.

THE YOUNG LIFE EQUIPPING ITSELF FOR GOD'S SERVICE: Sermons before the University of Cambridge. Sixth Edition. Extra fcap. 8vo. 3s. 6d.

THE SOLIDITY OF TRUE RELIGION; and other Sermons. Second Edition. Extra fcap. 8vo. 3s. 6d.

MEMORIALS OF HARROW SUNDAYS. A Selection of Sermons preached in the Chapel of Harrow School. Fifth Edition. Crown 8vo. 10s. 6d.

SERMONS IN HARROW SCHOOL CHAPEL (1847). 8vo. 10s. 6d.

NINE SERMONS IN HARROW SCHOOL CHAPEL (1849). Fcap. 8vo. 5s.

"MY SON, GIVE ME THINE HEART;" Sermons preached before the Universities of Oxford and Cambridge, 1876—78. Fcap. 8vo. 5s.

THE LORD'S PRAYER. Second Edition. Extra fcap. 8vo. 3s. 6d.

REST AWHILE: Addresses to Toilers in the Ministry. Extra fcap. 8vo. 5s.

TEMPLE SERMONS. Crown 8vo. 10s. 6d.

This volume contains a selection of the Sermons preached by Dr. Vaughan in the Temple Church during the twelve years that he has held the dignity of Master.

36 THEOLOGICAL BOOKS.

Vaughan (E. T.)—SOME REASONS OF OUR CHRISTIAN HOPE. Hulsean Lectures for 1875. By E. T. VAUGHAN, M.A., Rector of Harpenden. Crown 8vo. 6s. 6d.

Vaughan (D. J.)—Works by CANON VAUGHAN, of Leicester:
SERMONS PREACHED IN ST. JOHN'S CHURCH, LEICESTER, during the Years 1855 and 1856. Cr. 8vo. 5s. 6d.
CHRISTIAN EVIDENCES AND THE BIBLE. New Edition, revised and enlarged. Fcap. 8vo. 5s. 6d.
THE PRESENT TRIAL OF FAITH. Sermons preached in St. Martin's Church, Leicester. Crown 8vo. 9s.

Venn.—ON SOME OF THE CHARACTERISTICS OF BELIEF, Scientific and Religious. Being the Hulsean Lectures for 1869. By the Rev. J. VENN, M.A. 8vo. 6s. 6d.

These discourses are intended to illustrate, explain, and work out into some of their consequences, certain characteristics by which the attainment of religious belief is prominently distinguished from the attainment of belief upon most other subjects.

Vita.—LINKS AND CLUES. By Vita. Crown 8vo.

"*It is a long time since we have read a book so full of the life of a true spiritual mind. . . . Indeed, it is not so much a book to read through, as to read and return to as you do to the Bible itself, from which its whole significance is derived, in passages suited to the chief interest and difficulties of the moment. . . . . We cannot too cordially recommend a book which awakens the spirit, as hardly any book of the last few years has awakened it, to the real meaning of the Christian life.*"—The Spectator.

Warington.—THE WEEK OF CREATION; or, The Cosmogony of Genesis considered in its Relation to Modern Science. By GEORGE WARINGTON, Author of 'The Historic Character of the Pentateuch vindicated.' Crown 8vo. 4s. 6d.

Westcott.—Works by BROOKE FOSS WESTCOTT, D.D., Regius Professor of Divinity in the University of Cambridge; Canon of Peterborough:

The London Quarterly, speaking of Mr. Westcott, says—"To a learning and accuracy which command respect and confidence, he unites what are not always to be found in union with these qualities, the no less valuable faculties of lucid arrangement and graceful and facile expression."

AN INTRODUCTION TO THE STUDY OF THE GOSPELS. Fifth Edition. Crown 8vo. 10s. 6d.

The author's chief object in this work has been to shew that there is a true mean between the idea of a formal harmonization of the Gospels

THEOLOGICAL BOOKS. 37

WESTCOTT (Dr.)—*continued.*
and the abandonment of their absolute truth. After an Introduction on the General Effects of the course of Modern Philosophy on the popular views of Christianity, he proceeds to determine in what way the principles therein indicated may be applied to the study of the Gospels.

A GENERAL SURVEY OF THE HISTORY OF THE CANON OF THE NEW TESTAMENT during the First Four Centuries. Fifth Edition, revised, with a Preface on 'Supernatural Religion.' Crown 8vo. 10s. 6d.

The object of this treatise is to deal with the New Testament as a whole, and that on purely historical grounds. The separate books of which it is composed are considered not individually, but as claiming to be parts of the apostolic heritage of Christians. "*The treatise,*" says the British Quarterly, "*is a scholarly performance, learned, dispassionate, discriminating, worthy of his subject and of the present state of Christian literature in relation to it.*"

THE BIBLE IN THE CHURCH. A Popular Account of the Collection and Reception of the Holy Scriptures in the Christian Churches. Seventh Edition. 18mo. 4s. 6d.

A GENERAL VIEW OF THE HISTORY OF THE ENGLISH BIBLE. Second Edition. Crown 8vo. 10s. 6d.

The Pall Mall Gazette *calls the work "A brief, scholarly, and, to a great extent, an original contribution to theological literature."*

THE CHRISTIAN LIFE, MANIFOLD AND ONE. Six Sermons preached in Peterborough Cathedral. Crown 8vo. 2s. 6d.

THE GOSPEL OF THE RESURRECTION. Thoughts on its Relation to Reason and History. Fourth Edition, revised. Crown 8vo. 6s.

The present Essay is an endeavour to consider some of the elementary truths of Christianity, as a miraculous Revelation, from the side of History and Reason. The author endeavours to shew that a devout belief in the Life of Christ is quite compatible with a broad view of the course of human progress and a frank trust in the laws of our own minds. In the third edition the author has carefully reconsidered the whole argument, and by the help of several kind critics has been enabled to correct some faults and to remove some ambiguities, which had been overlooked before.

ON THE RELIGIOUS OFFICE OF THE UNIVERSITIES. Crown 8vo. 4s. 6d.

. . . . . . *There is wisdom, and truth, and thought enough, and a*

THEOLOGICAL BOOKS.

WESTCOTT (Dr.)—*continued.*
harmony and mutual connection running through them all, which makes the collection of more real value than many an ambitious treatise."—Literary Churchman.

Westcott—Hort.—THE NEW TESTAMENT IN THE ORIGINAL GREEK. The Text Revised by B. F. WESTCOTT, D.D., Regius Professor of Divinity, Canon of Peterborough, and F. J. A. HORT, D.D., Hulsean Professor of Divinity, Fellow of Emmanuel College, Cambridge: late Fellows of Trinity College, Cambridge. 2 vols. Crown 8vo. 10s. 6d. each.

Vol. I. TEXT. Vol. II. INTRODUCTION and APPENDIX.

"The Greek Testament as printed by the two Professors must in future rank as one of the highest critical authorities amongst English scholars."—Guardian.

"It is probably the most important contribution to Biblical learning in our generation."—Saturday Review.

"The object in view is to present the original words of the New Testament as nearly as they can be determined at the present time, to arrive at the texts of the autographs themselves so far as it is possible to obtain it by the help of existing materials. . . . . We attach much excellence to this manual edition of the Greek Testament, because it is the best contribution which England has made in modern times towards the production of a pure text. . . . It bears on its face evidences of calm judgment and commendable candour. The student may avail himself of its aid with much confidence. The Introduction and Appendix specially deserve minute attention."—The Athenæum.

Wilkins.—THE LIGHT OF THE WORLD. An Essay, by A. S. WILKINS, M.A., Professor of Latin in Owens College, Manchester. Second Edition. Crown 8vo. 3s. 6d.

"It would be difficult to praise too highly the spirit, the burden, the conclusions, or the scholarly finish of this beautiful Essay."—British Quarterly Review.

Wilson.—THE BIBLE STUDENT'S GUIDE TO THE MORE CORRECT UNDERSTANDING of the ENGLISH TRANSLATION OF THE OLD TESTAMENT, by Reference to the Original Hebrew. By WILLIAM WILSON, D.D., Canon of Winchester. Second Edition, carefully revised. 4to. 25s.

The author believes that the present work is the nearest approach to a complete Concordance of every word in the original that has yet been made; and as a Concordance it may be found of great use to the Bible student, while at the same time it serves the important object of furnishing the means of comparing synonymous words and of eliciting their precise and distinctive meaning. The knowledge of the Hebrew language is not absolutely necessary to the profitable use of the work.

THEOLOGICAL BOOKS.

Worship (The) of God and Fellowship among Men. Sermons on Public Worship. By Professor MAURICE, and others. Fcap. 8vo. 3s. 6d.

Yonge (Charlotte M.)—Works by CHARLOTTE M. YONGE, Author of 'The Heir of Redclyffe':

SCRIPTURE READINGS FOR SCHOOLS AND FAMILIES. 5 vols. Globe 8vo. 1s. 6d. With Comments, 3s. 6d. each.
FIRST SERIES. Genesis to Deuteronomy.
SECOND SERIES. From Joshua to Solomon.
THIRD SERIES. The Kings and Prophets.
FOURTH SERIES. The Gospel Times.
FIFTH SERIES. Apostolic Times.

Actual need has led the author to endeavour to prepare a reading book convenient for study with children, containing the very words of the Bible, with only a few expedient omissions, and arranged in Lessons of such length as by experience she has found to suit with children's ordinary power of accurate attentive interest. The verse form has been retained because of its convenience for children reading in class, and as more resembling their Bibles; but the poetical portions have been given in their lines. Professor Huxley at a meeting of the London School-board, particularly mentioned the Selection made by Miss Yonge, as an example of how selections might be made for School reading. "Her Comments are models of their kind."—Literary Churchman.

THE PUPILS OF ST. JOHN THE DIVINE. New Edition. Crown 8vo. 6s.

"*Young and old will be equally refreshed and taught by these pages, in which nothing is dull, and nothing is far-fetched.*"—Churchman.

PIONEERS AND FOUNDERS; or, Recent Workers in the Mission Field. With Frontispiece and Vignette Portrait of Bishop HEBER. Crown 8vo. 6s.

The missionaries whose biographies are here given, are—John Eliot, the Apostle of the Red Indians; David Brainerd, the Enthusiast; Christian F. Schwartz, the Councillor of Tanjore; Henry Martyn, the Scholar-Missionary; William Carey and Joshua Marshman, the Serampore Missionaries; the Judson Family; the Bishops of Calcutta—Thomas Middleton, Reginald Heber, Daniel Wilson; Samuel Marsden, the Australian Chaplain and Friend of the Maori; John Williams, the Martyr of Erromango; Allen Gardener, the Sailor Martyr; Charles Frederick Mackenzie, the Martyr of Zambesi.

THE "BOOK OF PRAISE" HYMNAL,

COMPILED AND ARRANGED BY

LORD SELBORNE.

In the following four forms:—

A. Beautifully printed in Royal 32mo., limp cloth, price 6d.
B. ,, ,, Small 18mo., larger type, cloth limp, 1s.
C. Same edition on fine paper, cloth, 1s. 6d.
Also an edition with Music, selected, harmonized, and composed by JOHN HULLAH, in square 18mo., cloth, 3s. 6d.

The large acceptance which has been given to "The Book of Praise" by all classes of Christian people encourages the Publishers in entertaining the hope that this Hymnal, which is mainly selected from it, may be extensively used in Congregations, and in some degree at least meet the desires of those who seek uniformity in common worship as a means towards that unity which pious souls yearn after, and which our Lord prayed for in behalf of his Church. "The office of a hymn is not to teach controversial Theology, but to give the voice of song to practical religion. No doubt, to do this, it must embody sound doctrine; but it ought to do so, not after the manner of the schools, but with the breadth, freedom, and simplicity of the Fountain-head." On this principle has Sir R. Palmer proceeded in the preparation of this book.

The arrangement adopted is the following:—

PART I. *consists of Hymns arranged according to the subjects of the Creed*—"*God the Creator,*" "*Christ Incarnate,*" "*Christ Crucified,*" "*Christ Risen,*" "*Christ Ascended,*" "*Christ's Kingdom and Judgment,*" *etc.*

PART II. *comprises Hymns arranged according to the subjects of the Lord's Prayer.*

PART III. *Hymns for natural and sacred seasons.*

There are 320 *Hymns in all.*

CAMBRIDGE: PRINTED BY J. PALMER.

www.ingramcontent.com/pod-product-compliance
Lightning Source LLC
Chambersburg PA
CBHW021401230426
43666CB00006B/601